A Pleasant Journey

A Memoir

By
Benjamin Kassogue

www.AuctusPublishers.com

Published by Auctus Publishers
606 Merion Avenue, First Floor
Havertown, PA 19083
Printed in the United States of America

ISBN : 979-8-9894812-1-7 (Print)
ISBN : 979-8-9894812-2-4 (Electronic)
Library of Congress Control Number: 2023950080

Contents

In memoriam to my father Elise Kassogue who is resting in the Lord Almighty's mercy

CHAPTER 1

A Rare Breed Woman

It had been a few months since I saw Mom since the last Christmas holidays. There she was, sitting under the towering nîme tree in front of her bedroom, reading her Bible. She has been and still is an avid reader of the Bible. I just got off the motorbike with my brother, who has been giving me a ride since I left the bus. As I approached her from the back, I saw by her left-hand side some of the plates, cups, and jugs she used earlier in the day. As soon as she looked back and saw me walking in her direction, she stood up and hurried towards me and welcomed me with a big bear hug, "Welcome home! Welcome home!"

"How was your trip?" she asked, "I see you are so tired."

"It was a long and exhausting trip," I said, "But I made it, and I feel wonderful."

I took this memorable trip to visit her in the village before traveling to the United States of America for graduate studies, and she was delighted to see me. Two days before I had planned to arrive for my visit to the village, she had asked my elder brother Esaie, who had been taking care of her in the town since Dad's demise, to go to meet me in Sevare, which is located in Mopti, the fifth region of Mali about seven hundred kilometers away from Bamako the capital city, and take me first to Dad's hometown, Medeli, for a short visit and to her hometown, Indelou, for another quick stop. Both villages are located in the region of Bandiagara nowadays. I arrived in Sevare and stayed the night at my brother's Gedeon house, who lives there with his family. The next day, Esaie drove up to Sevare.

When Esaie saw me, he smiled and asked, "Welcome! Are you excited about your first trip to your roots?"

"I am more than excited right now," I responded.

He said, "It will be a long journey with bumpy and crooked roads on the rocks."

"I am ready to face the challenge," I replied.

I climbed on Esaie's bike to take the trip. I have never had the chance to travel to my roots since birth. She wanted me to visit and learn more about my Dad's folks and uncles, walk in person on the ground, breathe the air, eat the food, drink the water, and glimpse how Dad lived while he was growing up. As Esaie said, the trip was long, and it became even longer when we had a puncture at one point in the journey and had to change the tire further down the road on another breakdown. We made it there in the late afternoon. My Dad's brother sat on a lounger in the middle of his compound. He received us gladly, "Welcome to your father's land."

"Thank you," I said.

"Your first time here won't be your last time," he inquired.

"I hope it won't be my last as well," I bellowed with a grin.

"How are you doing out here? We do not enjoy life as much as you over here." he smilingly complained, "Look at yourself, clean, neat, and well-bred. What are you eating there in the big city? You look like someone who never did farming activities."

I joked with him, "The same thing you eat over here."

Dad's people live in the highlands, which is the mountainous areas. The environment is good, the air is purer than in the big city where I live. The place are solid and built with stones and earth. Stone houses have a longer life, and I enjoyed discovering the beauty of the structure my Dad's people lived in. The houses are plastered with earth from the inside to seal the gaps. The walls are plastered from the outside to protect the building from rain and wind. The top part is also plastered. The roof is flat and built from wood covered with earth and plastic sheet. Each family building is ten to fifteen meters apart.

We were escorted by the firstborn from the eldest man's household to greet the different families of our relatives one after another. We had dinner at one of my uncles' houses and drove down to Sangha, a few kilometers down the road, to spend the night at a hotel. The hotel had nothing we could find in a routine and regular hotel. There was no bed, no running water, and no light. It only had worn-out mattresses. My brother and I took one of the mattresses to sleep on in the dark of one of the rooms.

From there, the following day, my brother took me to Mom's hometown, just a few kilometers away from Dad's. It is a small village located on the hills. We could not ride our motorbike into the village because, first, the mountain was too steep to climb with our bike, and second, the road had potholes, was up and down, and was too crooked for us to be able to ride our motorbike. It was too dangerous, and only the people who lived in the village knew how to navigate the roads. Mom's people were amicable and welcomed us with open arms. The structure of the buildings in the village looked the same as Dad's people.

The family chief, Mom's big brother, was proud to introduce us to every villager in the street. "Hello, you people over there! These guys are my sister Esther's children. The light-skinned one is her youngest, Benjamin, who lives in the big city of Bamako; the dark-skinned and tall one is Esaie, who lives with her in the village. They visited us today," he repeatedly told people while we walked around the village greeting." He later took us to the peak of the highest hills in the village. Before we climbed to the top, we stopped at the foot of the mountain to look at a giant tortoise in a little cave. The tortoise was so giant that one could sit on it the way one sits on the back of a donkey and put their legs on either side of the animal.

I asked, "Is it dangerous?"

My uncle said, "No, not all; if you give it something to eat, you can become its friend and sit on its back."

He warned, "If you sit on its back without giving it food while it is hungry, it will overthrow you on the rocky floor."

I looked at it carefully while he was peacefully having his lunch. I put my right hand on its tiled back, and it felt like I stroked it. We climbed up the hill. He took us to the very peak to see the fantastic view of the plain. We could see all the different villages a dozen kilometers away just by standing and looking down from the hill's peak. It was my first time, and I was awed by the beautiful view. Even though I liked the people and the place, we had to leave a few hours later. We went there in the middle of the day to head to Pomorododiou, where my Mom lived.

After greeting Mom and the rest of the family members, I washed in hot water heated by one of my nieces. I had lunch with the family in our big compound and spent the rest of the afternoon chatting with my nephews, nieces, and the neighbors who came to greet and praise God for keeping me safe since I last visited the village. In the evening, we had dinner and family prayer time as usual. This family prayer time is a regular solemn moment during which the family worships by singing songs and thanking God for His mercy, faithfulness, protection, love, and guidance. We thank Him for our successes and failures during the day, too. We also pray to God to further protect us from the devil and evil of the night and keep us under his protecting wings. After finishing the prayer, we bid goodbye to each other and join our bed. On this day, Mom, the prayer leader, had a long list of thanksgiving and intercession topics. She praised God for the blessings and mercies shown to the family since I last visited and other good things. She thanked God for things we generally take for granted, such as the ability to breathe, sleep, wake up sound and healthy, etc. She also presented the intercession topics and asked each one of us to pray for the healing of the sick in hospital or the outpatients, the protection of travelers inland or abroad, the employment of the unemployed, the security of the nation, the protection of the leaders and the led, etc. When we were done with the prayer, she took the floor to pronounce the blessings of the night. She always says the benefits at the end of every prayer time.

The following day, Mom called me over under the nîme tree to spend time together sometime after breakfast. She had her Bible next to her and had already jotted down many verses from the books of Exodus and Proverbs in her notebook. After some usual exchanges about how each of us had spent the night, Mom opened her Bible and read some passages out loud.

She said, "Please read the verses from the list I jotted down in my notebook."

"Do you understand the abbreviated book names?" she asked.

I looked at it and said, "The first is Proverbs, and the second is Exodus."

Even though I was unsure about the second one, she would chime in and ask some questions as I read from one chapter to another. When my answers were satisfactory, we would keep going. But when my answers to the questions were short or seemed unclear, she would pick up from this verse in the chapter and explain in a crystal clear manner what the passage meant. She purposely selected these two Books from the Bible. From the book of Exodus, Mom wanted me to know that I am already redeemed, and she also wanted me to understand the law, which gave instructions on how to be holy. From the book of Proverbs, she wanted me to understand the certainty of God's justice and the importance of prudence. She particularly stressed the central theme, "The fear of the Lord is the beginning of Knowledge." Even though I was almost thirty years old, she felt it was her role to keep helping me learn the importance of being raised in line with God's Words.

On the second day, Mom talked about how she and Dad met and got married, how they struggled in life, and how they eked out a living at the beginning while raising us, the children. Before meeting my Dad, her father and brother heard the Gospel from evangelists Ingelou Douyon and Bocar Saba. Baba Saba's father was a teacher at Notrosso's pastoral study school. His was of the Bozo ethnic group. Because of Mom's conversion to Christianity, she faced hatred from his kinsfolks. Two well-known figures, leaders, Mister Ndeogo Douyon (first Christian in Torou) and pastor Benjamin Poudiougou in Dankatene, who knew the danger associated with her being converted to Christianity, told her to flee to Sangha, where the American missionaries lived. The first objective of escaping to Sangha was to save her life, and the second was to study a,b,c,d (obtain literacy).

I wanted to hear more, "How and when did you get there?"

Mom responded, "I walked all the distance." First, I went to Somanagoro to meet another girl named Yamo so we could flee together."

She stopped momentarily. "When I arrived in Somanagoro, I got sick and stayed in bed for ten days."

"What happened then?" I asked.

Mom said, "After I recovered, we fled to Sangha; when we reached a village, it was nighttime. We spent the night at the village's pastor or chief of village's house."

"Did you pay them for staying the night at their place?" I asked.

"No, they offered us free accommodation," She said.

I was relieved, "that was nice of them."

"It was the standard of life; people at that time treated strangers kindly."

Sangha is located on the highland and is famous for its attractive tourist sites and housing the missionaries who traveled to Africa to spread the Gospel. A few weeks into her stay, Mom was forced to return to her Dad's village because the townspeople accused her Dad of selling her to the white men. A man was sent to Sangha to recover her. Mom said she started to cry when the man asked her to follow him. The missionary, Mister Bronze, and his wife consoled her and told her that she could flee again and return to Sangha because she still had the feet that she used to escape the first time. Mom followed the man to return to her Dad's village. They arrived at nighttime.

"What happened next?" I asked worryingly.

Mom said, "The same night, I was taken to another village called Dankatene, where my supposed fiancé was."

"I was put in a house, and the door was locked; the lock to the door was in wood, as was common during that time. The people who locked the door on me hung the key outside to allow my fiancé access to the room." she paused for a while, "I miraculously reached out to get the key and opened the door and freed myself."

"And then, did you return to your Dad's village?" I asked

She shouted, "No! Why would I do that? I jumped over the wall the same night to run to the village of Tourou to Mister Ndeogo Douyon's house."

"From there, I went to Sangha to resume my literacy," she concluded.

Dad was working as a servant to one of the missionaries whose name was Mister Balac. Mom and Dad met and fell in love. They got married with the help of the missionaries. Dad decided to undertake pastoral studies, and Mom followed him to Ntorosso in the Segou region. Ntorosso was the city where the religious study school was located and where many of the first pastors of the Dogon land studied. In the first year of their stay there, they had to trade off borrowing from the white men (pastoral school teachers) and provide them with small housework services. In the second year, they grew maize and fonio cereal during the rainy season to sustain themselves during the dry season. They eventually stopped borrowing and providing services to the white men. They grew more maize and fonio cereal in the following years to have enough for food and sell the rest to buy clothes and afford other necessities.

After the first three years of pastoral study, Dad was sent to Domounossogou as a trainee pastor. One of my sisters, Nema, means Grace, a name given by the church's women, was born there. It was the tradition that the church members gave the child the name. My parents honored the church women and let them give me the name Nema. Dad and Mom returned to Ntorosso for the second year, and Josue, the family's first male, was born there. Dad graduated from a pastoral study in the year 1959. During his services, Mom stayed with the kids while Dad occasionally traveled from village to village, evangelizing people and telling good tides to the pagans and or unbelievers.

Dad got transferred from one village to another for his services as Mom followed him. They spent two years in Tomotin. There were only a few believers in this village. It was the worst village Dad had ever lived in his entire pastoral mission.

"The village was full of witches and idolatry," Mom said, "Serpents were everywhere." She regretted, "Some people had them as pets, and others worshipped them."

But Mom also warned, "As pets, they kept the house at night. Thieves and wrongdoers could not enter the house at night; even visitors could not enter people's houses without their express permission."

Mom said, "The serpents would lie in front of the door and not let anybody into the house after a certain hour." When Dad was traveling, and Mom had a snake sneak into the compound, the village people refused to help her chase the snake away. She sought help from one of the few believers.

There were apes everywhere. During the rainy season, the apes were bothering them in their farming activities, and the harvest was unsatisfactory. Dad requested to be transferred to somewhere else and got transferred to Danadoungourou. David, the third of the family, was born in Dad's hometown, Medeli, when Dad returned there before going to Danadoungourou to serve as the primary pastor. David came into the world fragile and cost my parents a lot of resources.

"He was fragile, very sick, and was given no chance to survive," Mom recalled.

"Why?" I asked.

Mom said, "It is understandable because Dad and I were under tremendous pressure, and we struggled a lot in Tomotin, especially when I was pregnant with David due to the circumstances we lived in."

My parents, by God's Grace, through prayer and medication, were able to save his life. He grew up, got married, and had begotten four healthy and sound children before he died in 1995. Most of Dad's pastoral services were provided in Danadoungourou, where he spent twenty-four years. My other eight siblings and I were born and raised there. Luc and Jean, the twins Daniel, Gedeon, Enoc, Marie, Esaie, and Moise. Yes, twelve children, two daughters, and ten sons. Such a strong woman!

In the village, while growing up, I saw and witnessed Mom's love for and interest in helping people in need. It was in this village Mom helped women in the village to get literacy. She taught the women of the village activities such as making traditional soaps, frying beans, millet cakes, crushing ground peas, etc., to generate income. It was also in this village, Danadougourou, that she nursed an orphaned baby.

The reason why my father had begotten all of us is because he was the only child of my Grandpa (Deï). He was still very young when Grandpa passed away, and Grandma remarried to another man, leaving Dad with Grandpa's people. But his folks did not like him at all. He spent most of his time either caring for their animals in the bush or doing fieldwork for them on the family farm. He was scorned and hated by his people, who wanted him dead so they could own the lands belonging to my grandpa, lands that Dad had already inherited. He had no choice but to leave his people, who still live in the highland, to come down to the lowland and fend for himself and start a family.

Dad would say, "I will die one day. I will be gone, but my legacy will always be around you. They will carry my name and will never be forgotten."

"Does that mean they don't want to see us," I asked one day.

"They won't show it to you openly, but they are not your best friends," Dad said. "Whenever you travel there, don't sleep next to a wall. They will push the wall from behind to crush you."

"Do not accept food intended for you alone directly; instead, share food with them." Dad warned, "Eat together with them to save yourself from being poisoned."

"They are malicious these people," I feared.

"People will do anything to be landowners," Dad concluded.

Dad had already become a great-grandpa before he went to be with the Lord. I was proud of his achievement. That was why he made sure we bet on ourselves in life. He made sure we were workers and did everything efficiently in our life.

I was born in the lowland of the Bandiagara region (Mali, West Africa), in a village called Danadoungourou. I grew up in a family of twelve. I was given the name Benjamin at birth. It is a biblical name that means the "twelfth and youngest of the twelve tribes of Israel. In my case, the twelfth child of the Kassogue family. The Hebrew meaning is "son of the south" or "son of the right hand," from the roots (ben) meaning "son" (jamin) meaning "right hand, south." Benjamin alias Amagana, which means "Thank-you God." My parents gave me this name to show their gratefulness and recognition to God for blessing them with twelve (ten sons and two daughters) healthy and sound children. Dad never minded calling me with both names. Mom always called me by the latter. For her, every time she pronounced that name, it is one, to show her gratefulness to God, and two, for blessing her in her participation in the process of creating life. My parents are of the same ethnic group, "dogon" dialect group – "dono." My Father, Elisé Asseguem, came from Medeli, a village near the highlands in Bandiagara. He was among the fourth or fifth-generation pastors (religious leaders and scholars) of the Dogon land. He studied the Bible with the American missionaries and was one of the best students of the Bible school (as mentioned in his diploma) and top among his cohorts. He was awarded with two others in the cohort the merit prize, one of whom was his best friend and colleague, Late Pastor Asseguem Kodio. Dad and Papa Asseguem Kodio continued to be very close friends for the rest of their lives. Their friendship brought the two families together and they both knew each other's family like the palm of their hand. Dad and Papa Asseguem Kodio worked closely, perfectly performed their mission and went on to teach the Bible from cover to cover and probably the maps in it.

Dad was a very tall, about six feet four, dark-skinned, and handsome man. He was a soft-hearted person for us children his offspring, but he was strict about our needs to study, learn, and be successful. He was the one who first taught us how to read and write. He was the first teacher of all his children. A few months before the school year started, he used to call one of us, who was at school, and taught him how to spell, read, and write. What I liked best when my turn came around to be registered in school was the writing practice because he held my hand and taught me how to write numbers and letters of the alphabet on the sandy floor using my index finger.

"Let your finger go, and I got it. Let it depend on my hand," he would order.

"The number "three" was the most difficult for me to write," I would struggle.

Dad would explain, "The number three is similar to the capital letter "E" when you turn it the other way around."

He accompanied me on the first day of school, holding my hands in his. He exchanged some words with the principal and with some of the teachers who were at school early. Then he left after wishing me good luck. It was in his habits to accompany his children on the first day of school, exchange with a few teachers, and wish them luck.

Seeing his commitment to his children's schooling needs, some teachers befriended him and paid him a visit on some weekends.

"It is not very often one sees a parent like you nowadays," said the principal of the middle school I was attending during one of his visits.

Dad was pleased with his remarks, "I do my best to help them embrace life's challenges."

The principal told my father, "Though Benjamin is in the eighth grade, I do not doubt that he would excel in the ninth grade if put there."

"I am happy to hear that," Dad proudly said.

Dad valued truth, honesty, justice, and integrity in his lifetime. He was a very loving head of the family and a protective and caring father to his children. He mainly slept during the day. As he used to say after lunch, "Let me have a nap." At night, he generally slept during the early hours of the night. That allowed him to be awake as the night wore on.

Some of the neighbors used to say, "That pastor next door never sleeps at night; he is always on the lookout."

Dad owned a comfortable lounger that he would lie on in front of the house's main entrance. Sometimes, he spent the entire night lying on the lounger to look after his family. It was lying on the lounger that, one night, he caught a man who wanted to sneak into the house. It happened during the autumn and just before school started. Most of us children were asleep inside the house that night, and one of my brothers, Jean, a teacher in another town, was visiting with his wife and their baby son. We all spent the day talking, eating, and laughing. It was some getting-together, a type of family reunion. That night, he had slept during the day as usual and was lying on the lounger a few feet away from a massive tree called "Kumu" in front of our house.

Around two in the morning, he saw a figure moving in the dark, in the shade of the vast, tall tree. He would always say that two to three in the morning is the moment when wrongdoers do their business and shenanigans. This is the moment when many people are deep into their sleep. The moonlight made it so that it was not very dark because the moonbeam crossed the leaves of the enormous tree, which allowed my father to see that someone was walking towards the house's entrance. He waited until the man walked very close, a couple of yards away, and flashed his lamp at his face while still lying on the lounger. He always had his lamp by his lounger and charged with the newest battery he had bought at the shopkeepers'. The lamp's light was so bright that the man was blinded and stood still there. He was vibrating, shaking, his heart pounding, and sweat running down his forehead.

Dad questioned him, "Who are you, and what are you looking for?"

He answered, "I am ...bubbling... I am looking for direction."

He added, "I am coming from a neighboring village and am going to another neighboring town."

It was a lousy lie; my father knew it, and the man himself understood it. A bare-handed man traveling from one village to another at this hour of the night was curious. He was ashamed of the lie himself. He had nowhere to hide. My father could have hunted him down and alerted the family and the neighbors and would have shamed him in front of the neighbors and everyone. Dad was not the type of man who liked shaming people for whatever reason. He found it not wise to shame people, even if he was right.

Dad told the man, "The way to get to the village you are supposedly heading for is the other way around."

He kept his lamp light on in that direction until the man turned round to walk back and around the street's corner. He then followed the man a hundred yards from behind until the man left the village.

When Dad told the story to the rest of the family the following day, my brother Jean could not believe it.

He was disappointed, "Why did you not wake me up, Dad?" "I could have dealt with that man in the middle of the night."

Jean had a shotgun to protect his family and carried it with him during his trips.

He assured, "I would at least have scared the wits out of him with this shotgun."

But it was not to be. Dad said, "First, I did not want to disturb you, and second, I wanted to use him as a messenger to others who might be considering breaking into this house at night." While laughing, Dad added, "He will tell the other ill-willed people who might come to our house that I am always on the lookout; it will dissuade them." My father would not let that happen.

Even after he retired from his pastoral duties, he stayed his old self in his old age. He cared for his household as much as when still serving complete responsibilities. In the final years of his pastoral duties, a house was being built on the outskirts of the village where the family moved in after Dad had retired. The family had initially moved some possessions to the new house, such as carts, rarely used items, and even some animals, such as cows, sheep, goats, hens, roosters, etc. Dad was going forth and back between the new house and the house we lived in then. Frequently, he would go to the new place to watch after the animals by midnight and stay there until the early hours of the morning. Sometimes, he would also go there during the day, relax for two or three hours, and enjoy the quietness and peace of the outskirts. Other times, he would randomly drop by there to check on everything.

One evening, as he was doing his usual thing, he caught a man from the village stealing one of our roosters. This man knew my family well, and everybody knew him. He was well known by almost everyone else in the village because he was used to selling meat to the villagers. He even used to bring his meat to our house so my mother could buy it. My father and the man, with the rooster in his hands, met at the very entrance of the house like clapping hands. They both stared at each other for some time. My father then walked, bypassed him, and went inside the compound. What happened next was unheard of. This man turned round, walked back inside the compound to put the rooster back on the chicken coop by the nîme tree, and walked out of the house with heads down and tail between legs. He did something incredible; he went on to tell the people in the village about his monstrous deed. He even went to see some people at the blacksmith's shop to tell them about his wrongdoing and asked them to ask for forgiveness from my father. My Dad did not say a single word about it to anyone in the village. He did not even tell the family about what happened on that night. The family members heard about it from the gossiping of the village people.

Dad's care, love, and sacrifice for his family was truly unmatched. He would study each of us on a daily basis through our attitude, mood, gesture, gait, look, speech, hearing etc. which allowed him to know if we were healthy, sound, fit, and sane. When cholera became an epidemic in the nineties Dad was on alert every day, all day. Since cholera is a water borne disease, Dad would deliberately wake up in the middle of the night, when everyone else was asleep, to bleach the water in the drinking water pot by dropping the recommended drops into each pot. Mom caught him while he was doing so and told us the next morning. We were pleasantly surprised seeing how far he would go for his family. He made sure that every dredge of water in the drinking water pot was cholera bacteria free.

He was truthful and was astonished about how humanity is almost devoid of truthfulness. He showed his disappointment by always saying this phrase: *"Ine goro ku taï dinyan arakara iyèrè giyatiye woï yèdaga"* that is to say, "If somebody lies down flat on his back and says that he does not see the sky, just leave him alone." No one is as blind as the one who does not want to see.

He was a lightning rod and was very famous for speaking his mind. His critical remarks made him a ruffler of feathers in society. One occasion, during the yearly service work for the community, he went hard on some greedy folks who wanted to eat a big piece of meat that fell behind either a random butcher or a meat carrier. On a service work day, people gathered and walked down to the village pond to work the mud used to plaster the church wall. During the walk to the pond, a group of people from the multitude discovered a few kilograms of meat left on the ground. They gathered it and wanted to use it for lunch. This action did not go down well with Dad. He told these people that they were too greedy. He said, "You are an abject meat slave."

"You are obsessed with meat," he yelled.

"Are you desperate to this point?" he asked, shaking his head.

Some elders agreed, "You, young people today, do not love yourself."

One of the elders was too disappointed, "You are suicidal if you are going to eat this meat."

Dad could not understand why they were too much into the meat. He wondered what was wrong with them. If people could not resist the temptation to use a random piece of meat for lunch, they had no qualms. That was how he thought of these people. Following this event, some people in the community started calling my Dad using the expression "people are obsessed with meat." It became a reminder for people to be wary of loose meat. Whenever people see my Dad far away walking, they say, "people are obsessed with meat; aren't you ashamed of yourself?" It has become some nickname.

As the youngest, I had the privilege to share the three meals of the day with my Dad. In my culture, it is infrequent to see the father of the house sharing meals altogether with the rest of the family. Mom usually puts Dad's dinner in a specific place and a personalized container. He generally had meals alone, but when I was five or six, he requested that I have meals with him from that point onward, and Mom accepted. Since then, I always had dinner with him. We had a specially structured mealtime. I would sit facing Dad with the dish between us in the middle. On either side of the plate, we would have a hand washing kit and drinking water cup on a small stool, water we would drink after eating. The hands-washing water container would sit on the right side of Dad, and the drinking water jug on his left side.

He would wash his hands first and pass it to me. I would wash my hands using the same water. Washing my hands with the same water he used further strengthened our bond. Then, he would praise and thank God for the meal before cutting the first toast. He would pray along this line, *"Thank you, God, for blessing us. Bless our food and drink. Since you redeemed us so dearly and delivered us from evil, as you gave us a share in this food, so may you give us a share in eternal life, Amen!"*

I would wait until he would start to chew his first toast before getting mine. I would hold the container the entire time we had food; holding the plate while eating is a sign of respect for and gratitude to parents or those who have provided the food. After we finished, I would take the dish back to Mom in front of the kitchen and pour the hand-washing water on the floor outside in front of the main entrance. The bond between Dad and me was so strong that I felt his transfer to heaven a few months before. In the months preceding his death, I would wake up every night in the middle of the night, stay awake for a couple of hours, and then fall back asleep. At first, I thought it was the tea I was taking during the day, so I stopped it but in vain. I could not understand why this was happening to me until his death. After his death, I started sleeping as usual. The bond between us was so deep!

He was a sincere human being. Honesty is compelling. He used to say, "The more honest one is, the better off one is, and the more respect one will have," he repeatedly said. He was truthful and wanted all his offspring to be sincere in every way possible, no matter where and when. He never tried to deceive people for personal gain, even if it meant bad news for him. He was a lawful man as well. He believes that even Almighty God wants us to abide by laws. He always highlighted how the scripture recommends respecting the law in his preaching. According to the Bible, we cannot respect God's laws if we cannot appreciate the rules we have passed (our own laws). A long time (eight years) after he went to be with the Lord, I met a man who resembled my father in many aspects of life. That man later became a mentor figure to me. His name is GEITHER. He is truthful, honest, transparent, charismatic, self-controlled, etc.

MISTER GEITHER is one of the most unique personalities one can ever meet in one's lifetime. My trip to America was an eye-opening opportunity and also a learning opportunity. Two weeks after my arrival to the United States for my higher education endeavors, my host Mom took me to her church for the first time. "The Berean Baptist Church". It used to be a big church even though there was no full-time Pastor. It is located at 4822 North Vancouver Ave, Portland, Oregon 97217. The church had a heating system but not a cooling system, which means that during the summer, when it got really hot, standing fans were brought in during Sunday service to cool down the place to allow faithful worshippers to have a peaceful service. The church had only a couple of dozen believers, but they were firm believers who stayed loyal to the church even though it did not have a full-time pastor.

A couple of months later, I got more involved in church life. I started collecting tithe, working as a greeter on some Sundays, and even running the sound system. I also took care of the church lawn. I mowed the church's lawn every week to keep the church attracted to passersby and the people in the community. MISTER GEITHER is one of the unique personalities one can only meet once in one's lifetime. He is known as "Ron" for short. He was the church's president when I attended and even after I left. I saw something special in him since my first day at the church. MISTER GEITHER was an average-age man with dark skin. He used to cut his hair uniquely, though I disliked it. It was a nice haircut. He cut the hair on the lower part of his head shorter than the upper part. This allowed him to comb the upper part to cover the shorter part, making his hair look like the wilting/drooping leaves. It is called a "combed down fringe full wig."

I thoroughly appreciated this man during my two-year stay at this church. I even told him I would name my son after him, though I was still a single man. The church occasionally allowed men to have breakfast at one the most excellent restaurants in downtown Portland. The one I can recall was called McMenamins. But once we went for breakfast to another restaurant whose name I do not remember now. On that day, I noticed some of the waitresses dressed very provocatively. I had already found out that MISTER GEITHER has incredible self-control when it comes to speech through our everyday conversations. He is very selective in his words and says what needs to be said (the right thing). For instance, he would say I was going to say this, but I will say this; that was what I was thinking, but I realized I needed to say this instead.

I looked around the dining table when we were at the restaurant for breakfast. I realized that almost everyone in the group had at least looked twice or more at the waitresses carrying the menu and dressed provocatively. MISTER GEITHER, my target, when the waitress reached him, he took the menu, made his choice, and gave the menu back to her without looking at her. We see for the first time, but the second time, we look, and we look with intention. With intention, we develop desires. Desires will soon become a behavior. Behavior will lead to a habit, which is synonymous with practice. Practice will inevitably make it nature; your nature is simply who you are.

Dad has always enjoyed the challenges of raising children and has spoken of his experience fondly and shared it with us on multiple occasions. According to him, it is worth organizing a party when a human has matured and has become an adult. Childhood and adolescenthood include one the most challenging behaviors and a million steps to cross by children and parents. While Mom played her role ideally during the child's developmental stage, Dad kicked in during adolescenthood.

"It is the period in which a father figure showed his leadership and disciplinarian role," Dad said.

The childhood/adolescent period is very daunting for committed parents. It is so challenging, wearing down, and tiresome for children and parents that organizing a big party to celebrate the transition from childhood/ adolescenthood to adulthood is worth organizing. It takes the whole community to bring up a child/an adolescent. Children belong to everyone, and it is community-oriented and geared to solving the community's problems. Young children were therefore raised in how to contribute to the community's social life to prepare them to fit into their community. That is why Dad was not in the mood to come to your defense when you came home crying or sobbing. He would first ask you what you did wrong out there. If you are calling for being rebuked, scolded, or beaten, he would say there are plenty of children out there, and you are the only one who got beat, scolded, and rebuked; you must have done something wrong. He would further blame, scold, or beat you up if he found out that was the case. Dad always expected us to show others the respect and commitment we have shown him and Mom. "People would know whether you received a good education through your everyday behavior and attitude."

He usually said, "Your everyday attitude and behavior will show the kind of education you received from your parents."

He always required and reminded us, "Go out and be the best version of yourself and equivalent to the education you obtained from me and Mom."

In the late 1950s, when Dad graduated from Bible School, Dad turned into clothes the cotton that Mom had smoothed and spun into threads. Mom did the first part of the cotton work at night after working for the missionary teachers as a maid during the day. Dad did the cotton work in the evening or at night because, during the day, he had to attend classes. When the cotton was processed to turn it into clothes, Dad would take them to the marketplace to sell it. The cycle would start over again.

Dad was a very hard-working man. He worked so hard that he could feel blood, sweat, and smell blood. Around the final year of pastoral study before his stay for religious services in Tomotin and Danadoungourou after he graduated, Dad and Mom worked relentlessly. Dad had an issue going on with him. He had intense and sometimes almost unbearable pain in his lower belly part. Working and turning the cotton into clothes while sitting for hours did not help either. Farming with hands and hoes only worsened the pain. During the break from farming to have breakfast or lunch, Dad could not sit on his buttocks; the pain was too much. He had to lie down on his left or right side to eat. With the help of the Christian missionaries, he visited a hospital in Bandiagara, where he had sixty injections. One of the missionaries' wives, a medical practitioner, told Dad that he had muscle tears in his lower belly and recommended that he does not lift any load requiring some strength. Afterward, he was told to drink a lot of water and continue to have stenciling shots whenever he felt the pain again.

While serving in Tomotin and the early years of his stay in Danadoungourou, Dad bought old bicycles from young people who traveled to Cote d'Ivoire during the dry season for green pasture. He repaired and sold the repaired bicycles to make profits. Many young people traveled back and forth to Cote d'Ivoire and the neighboring countries for a better life. These young people come back from adventure with new bicycles. They would use the bicycle for a while, sell it, and use the money to travel to green pastures for more again. Dad would buy the old bicycles and make business profits.

He firmly believed in agriculture and regularly said, "It would pay cash if you put the hard work in."

"Mother Earth will produce very well if you allow it to do so by working it the appropriate way and giving it the right amount of dirt to make it fertile," Dad assured, "She is very trustworthy; give her what she needs and wait and see her fruits."

"I want to learn to work hard," I always said and reminded myself of that sentence to myself.

Dad never wanted to move to big cities, even when he had the opportunity to do so. For him, living in a big city made agricultural activities more difficult because farming lands were scarce, they were far away, lands were more challenging to access, and children were more interested in city life and city attractions than farming. We had plenty of farming land in the village and cultivated all of them during the rainy seasons. Dad and Mom practiced agriculture with hands only. They grew peanut, fonio, dah, millet, maize, sorghum, beans, etc., which contributed to purchasing the sewing machine, the motorbike, the kart, and the plowshare. Dad raised all of us mainly with their farming products, too. He was the first person to teach agricultural practices and techniques to many men in the village of Danadoungourou.

He learned farming techniques from the area's agents of water and forests. He bought the plow and the kart on the recommendation of these agents. The agent told him, "The plow and kart go together. You cannot buy one and not the other." Buying the plow alone meant one had to carry it on their head. So, Dad got both, but he had to make the wood of the kart himself. He would go into the field to cut dead trees and carve them into wood until he got enough.

One day, Dad stayed too late in the field, and Mom was worried. When he finally came home in the evening, he was carrying an injury in his shin. He had accidentally cut his shin deep, and it was bleeding nonstop. Mom had already fixed dinner and told Dad to have dinner and let her take care of the wound. She took the package that contained permanganate and mercurochrome and helped wash the wound until it stopped bleeding.

"Was Dad a health practitioner then?" I asked.

"No," Mom said, "Then he did not practice medical services. He learned that later."

At that time, many practiced farming with hands and hoes only. Only a select few could afford the plow. Dad was one of the first to buy one. It was a strong, heavy, and well-built plow. He used it to help other farmers do farming by showing them the techniques of tying the oxen, camels, or donkeys to pull it during the growing season. Thanks to him, many people could master the proper spacing techniques and the seedling of plants.

Dad also was the doer of other activities like sewing; he was a tailor and health practitioner. He owned sewing machines such as Singer and Bernina. Dad bought a sewing machine one year after he bought the motorbike. He was very good at cutting and sewing. All women and men from the village and neighboring villages brought their clothes to be sewn. We children never worried about clothing after Dad bought the sewing machine. He sewed clothes for all of his children. We always had our clothes a week or two weeks before the D-day during Christmas and Easter. Dad was sometimes too busy sewing. One day, he badly hurt his finger while sewing. The sewing machine needle pierced his index finger all the way through. It was a horrendous injury. His finger was bleeding like a broken nose for a long time before he succeeded in pulling out the thread that was inside his finger. After pulling out the thread, he put some alcohol and permanganate. He bandaged it and went ahead with his sewing tasks.

As a health practitioner, he cared for our children when we became sick. He would first take us to the health center and carefully follow instructions from the doctor about the prescriptions and the injections. He would do exactly as the doctor asked regarding the time, dosage, etc. He would also take care of the village people and people from the neighboring villages. At the time, the injections were made with the same needle repeatedly. Dad would always pasteurize the previously used needle by boiling it with water and alcohol before using it again with a new patient. Dad comforted the patients who would come to receive injections that they did not have to fear.

"After the needle had pierced the dark skin, you don't feel any pain." He would say. Dad also made injections to himself when he became sick. It was the scariest thing I experienced as a child. He would go into the bathroom, inject himself, and get out as if nothing had happened there.

I was so bewildered, "Have you made the injection to yourself?"

"Of course, it is simple," he always responded.

I was always amazed when Dad made self-injection.

He also had black stones for snake bites. When people came to him for snake bites, he would apply the black stone called Nagamani to treat the snake bites. The black stone was used to soak up the poison at the entry point. The stone was placed on the skin, and a small cut was made on the bitten area until blood oozed. The stone then absorbs the poison through capillary action, reducing the fatality of the snake bite. When Dad applied the stone, which soaked up the blood and fell, he would apply another until the black stone did not stick to the cut area. He used milk and hot water to pasteurize the stone that soaked up the venom before the subsequent cases of snake bites were reported.

Multiple decades after he started working as a health practitioner, I was told about Dad's fantastic work using black stones. I became so curious about the black stone. One day, in second grade, I started playing with a classmate while sitting at one of the windows. The wind blew hard and slammed the window against my index finger, and a dangling tiny iron pierced an opening on my finger. After school, when I returned home to show Dad the piercing on the finger.

He asked restlessly, "What happened to your finger?"

And I said, "I put my finger into a hole inside the second-grade classroom."

"Did it bleed?" he requested, looking at it painstakingly

"Just a little bit," I said.

"Is it swelling?" he asked again with the same look.

Again, I said "No". Dad was relaxed.

I was scared to tell Dad or Mom that I was playing while sitting on the window when it happened. Dad and Mom always told me to pay attention and not mess around when the teacher was not in the classroom. They would have scolded me if I had told them the truth because I was advised against it. Dad accompanied me to the school, said the second-grade teacher, Monsieur Banri (white teacher). We called him so in the village because he had light skin and was nomadic.

When we arrived, Dad shook hands with him and said, "Could you please open the door to the classroom? My son is injured and said he put his finger in a hole. I want to see the hole myself."

Once inside, Dad asked, "Where is the hole?"

I responded, "Over there in the corner." Dad and Monsieur Banri inspected it for a while.

Monsieur Banri said, "It was probably a mouse that bit him," He assured, "There are no snakes in this school."

Dad said, "It does not look like a snake bite," but asked me, "Do you want me to apply the black stone?"

And I said "Yes".

But the stone fell a few hours later. Dad never understood what happened to my finger. I never told him or anyone what happened.

When Mom gave birth to twins in the nineteen sixties, my twin brothers Luc and Jean, the committee of the pastors with whom Dad worked said that Dad would struggle more in life from then on. They firmly believed "The birth of the twins would be the harbinger of his downfall financially. Now you are pedaling a bicycle to events; later, you will walk to events." They said, "Raising twins is much harder for parents." But Dad and Mom defied the odds and became better off instead. During a ceremony organized to show gratefulness to God for the twins in the presence of some of the committee members, a friend of Dad brought the motorbike home. They could not believe their eyes. Only a few people owned or had the money to buy a Motobecane in the village then. Dad only used the motorbike to travel long distances and on special occasions. On special events, such as wedding ceremonies in another village, he would meet other pastors coming for the same purpose. He also rode the motorbike to attend biannual Christian gatherings at the district level. The motorbike was also used for emergencies for the family and the people of the village. When a family member got sick or seriously injured, Dad would take the victim to the health center as quickly as possible to treat them. When some people in the village also got sick late at night, and it was severe, they would come to ask Dad for help, and Dad would either take the person to the health center or ask one of my brothers to take the trip.

Over the years, Dad became so good at driving the motorbike. He was very agile, cautious, and very experienced. He would be going and looking at the roadside sometimes. You see him facing the side of the road and looking, but he was also aware of what was happening ahead of the road. We, children, would talk about it whenever he traveled with the motorbike and laughed our heads off. Whenever I watch MotoGP and the Dakar Rally, I think about my Dad. One day, we children were returning home from the farms, and Dad was riding to some location for reasons we ignored. He was looking towards us. He was looking at some animals in the field between us and did not notice a donkey pulling a kart right before him. When he realized he was too close to the kart to stop, he swerved to the left and lifted his right leg to hover over the top to prevent his leg from hitting the side of the kart and hurting himself.

He was so good at driving the motorbike. In my recollection, he had only two unfortunate accidents. First, he was driving from an annual meeting on a sandy road. After riding for about an hour and a half, he was tired, and the sand was too much. He fell and had bruises all over his body. On the second one, he was called to pray for a sick person in a neighboring village. He left the house at about two in the afternoon, and five minutes later, he was taken out by a careless motorist driving in the village's streets. When we were alerted, and I arrived at the scene, Dad sat on a chair. A villager in front of whose house the accident happened brought the chair so that he could be seated on it. I crawled in front of Dad and had tears running down my cheeks in double lines. Mom also ran up there and was stopped by the women in the neighborhood who had gathered a few yards from where the accidents happened. They stood in a circle around Mom to console her. Many of the women were telling her not to worry a little bit. I bet these women did not know anything about the seriousness of the accident. They were not close enough to see Dad suffering. They were just optimistic, I guessed. They assured Mom that Dad would be okay because he was a strong and resilient man. Someone was asking Dad where he had pain, and Dad was sitting there with little reaction. He was lost in his thoughts.

A few minutes later, the vehicle owner offered to take Dad to the hospital in Koro, the capital city of our administration division. Mom was allowed to take the trip to the hospital with them. There was no such thing as an ambulance. Dad stayed in the hospital for a few days and was released. Mom came home first, and Dad came home later with one of my brothers riding him home. He was sound, healthy, and ready to go again. He started his usual business of riding, sewing, and caring for his family. Even though he complained here and there about some pain, and we would apply the lotion prescribed by the doctor, he was okay overall.

When it came to agriculture, all the grown-up children were involved in the sowing and farming activities. The sowing activities take place in June of every year. It is the beginning of the rainy season. After the first heavy summer rain, all the community members go out in their fields to put the first seeds into the soil. Dad would accompany us in this activity and play a supervising role. Sowing, which consists of putting the seeds into the wet soil after being cut open by a long special hoe, lasted for about two to four days and even six if the family had many farms. It is a very tiring and exhausting task. For us, the sowing took two days minimum, most years.

When we were at the farm, one or two of us would cut the soil open with the long hoe made for that purpose, and the rest of us would put the seed in the opening and close it with our bare feet. You are not allowed to wear shoes while doing that. Dad would closely follow us to see if we put the right amount of seed in the ground and if the openings were well closed to allow the sprouting. The seeds were sometimes mixed with fertilizers to allow better growing and powder pesticide to prevent insects from eating or spoiling them. Dad's careful attention enabled him to know who was doing a good job and who was not. He would also know if some of us put too many seeds in one hole. If your cup was getting empty quicker than the other's cup and you were working equally with the others, Dad would tell you, "You are using too many seeds in relation to the scope of your work." It was common for Dad to call out someone in the afternoon of the first day or on the second day of sowing when tiredness kicked in.

He would call you by your name and encourage you, "Put in the effort, stay focused!" Occasionally, some of us would spill the seeds from the small container, which Dad hated. He would warn the person spilling only once or a maximum of twice. "Hold your container carefully, guys. You have special seeds in it which would provide food for next year," he would plead.

That was his final verdict. If one spilled the seeds again following the first warning (s), Dad would ignore you and say nothing. He would continue doing his part of the work and make you feel he was unaware of you spilling the seeds. He would wait until he got close to you. He would slap you hard when he gets close enough; your face would light up before going completely dark. After that, you would wake up and see clearly.

"Never spill the seeds again," he would threaten, "pull it together!"

The farming activities happened from mid-June to August. Dad visited the blacksmith in late April or early May to pay them to make enough hoes and other equipment used in the upcoming farming season and for the harvesting activities from September to December. Most of the hoes he made were small and easy to handle during farming. We generally had no problem holding the hoes, but as in every work, accidents happened. Some of us would cut the flat of our foot with the hoes.

When this happened, Dad would say to the person, "If you had a good grip on the hoe while farming, this would not happen to you."

"Maybe you were tired or lost focus for a fraction of a second."

As a health practitioner, he would clean the wound with alcohol, apply some mercurochrome, and bandage it. The next day, you would go to the farm with the others as usual. You are "*our ani*," meaning you are a strong man, a warrior! He told us that when he was a kid and accidentally cut the flat of his foot, he would put some fine sand in the fresh wound and keep farming. He said: "The iron of the hoe has been plowing the land for quite a while, and it has no tetanus in it."

We went to the farm as early as six o'clock in the morning. Dad always encouraged us to be at the farm as early as possible in the morning.

"The world belongs to those who wake up early," or "the early bird catches the worm," he would say most mornings before we left for the farm.

"Go out there and work as hard as you can," he would recommend.

We were so committed to working hard and finishing the farming work as quickly as possible that we stayed on the farm even if it rained and started working right after the rain had stopped.

But Dad said, "Rain never disturbs farming work. It is because of the rain that the plants flourish."

He would order, 'Stop farming and return home because it is safer to be home than on the farm."

He would say, "Tomorrow is another day."

Every time it rained heavily in the morning or during the day and we children were home; Dad would ask Mom to make hot coffee for all of us. We would have the hot coffee and leave for the farm in the morning or relax for the rest of the day when it was too late in the afternoon to go to the farm.

Since we had multiple farms, Dad would visit the farm we had already finished farming and check out our work. He did that every time we worked at each farm and reported his observations and remarks to us. After visiting, he would wait until the next day to proudly tell us that we did a great job at that farm. He would add that he did not worry about us, his children, because all of our farming work met his expectations or sometimes was above his expectations, and he had no concern that we would be fine in every aspect of life if we continued working the way we did at the farm.

Dad was also a prominent breeder of animals, and he loved animals. He bred animals like oxen, donkeys, sheep, and goats for agriculture or sale purposes, and he also had many of them. Some of the animals, he bought them when they were little and bred them until they started reproducing, especially the rams. Others, like good brood goats and sheep, when they were old enough to speed up the reproduction process. The breeding of these animals also contributed a lot to Dad's financial state. He took outstanding care of animals.

He said, "The animals, especially the oxen, helped in the growing season by pulling the plow during farming activities."

He genuinely believed, "If you take good care of animals like oxen, donkeys, camels, and horses, they would do sixty percent of the farming on your behalf by plowing."

People had to work between the lines made by the plowing done by animals. Once, we had a dark ox that was very lean and slender. Dad gathered all sorts of good leaves, herbs, and quality animal food available for it to eat. It would remain skinny even after eating those unique leaves, herbs, and food. Dad wondered why the ox was not getting fat like the other oxen we had. He was unsuccessful in helping the ox get fat. One day, while farming, I used the ox to plow with my nephew, pulling the leash at its neck. After plowing and making a few lines, the ox refused to pull in as I wanted. So, I tried to whip it. It was so afraid of being hit and started to jump all over the place. I lost control, and it stepped on the ploughshare. The blade cut the back of its right rear foot. The cut was so deep, and it was bleeding hell. I asked my nephew, caring for the oxen, to take it home to Dad for treatment. In the evening, when I got home, Dad was unhappy.

He asked, "What happened at the farm today?"

"The ox became too lazy after plowing a few lines," I responded with fear and anxiety.

Dad said, looking me in the eyes, "I told you not to force the animal if it refused to pull the plow; it means the animal is tired or not feeling well." He complained, "You should have given a break to the animal for twenty to thirty minutes instead of trying to force it."

"I understand," I said with a low voice, "next time, I will not force it."

"Too late for that now; it will not be able to plow for the next few months. You will have to use the other two oxen only," Dad said.

In cases, Dad was with us on the farm for whatever reason, and the oxen would refuse to pull the plow; he would threaten the oxen with a small tree branch to make it do the plowing. He would whip in the air to noise-threaten the animal; if the threat were adequate, the animal would resume plowing; if not, the animal would not, and Dad would tell us to take a break. The donkey was used to pull the karts and water from the well for the family's needs. In the village, the wells were thirty to forty meters deep, so it was necessary to use the donkeys whenever a large quantity of water was needed. The goats and sheep were bred to be sold, and the money was used to pay family expenses.

Sometimes, it was difficult for us to care for the animals, do farming activities, and do other household tasks. When school was about to start, and nobody was available to take care of the animals, Dad would have us take them to a remote village for the Fulani people so they could take care of them. Once, I was asked to take the animals with the help of a shepherd to a remote village. I was not very comfortable to accompany him in taking the animals there. I traveled with him to spend a night there before returning. It was the most extended trip of my life. The place these people lived had only a makeshift hut. They had a big log burning all the time to keep themselves from the cold, and the fire on the record never went out. Their food was tasteless and unhealthy. One night I spent there, they gave me fresh milk for the sauce with the millet dough they had made for dinner. I could not eat the sauce they cooked, and it was sour.

When I returned to the village, I shared the story with Mom. She pointed her index straight to my face and said, "See? Right there, that is your problem," When Mom points her index finger right to your face, she means some profound lessons. "I am disappointed in you, Amagana," referring to me using my second name. "You need to become a strong man. You cannot find as sweet as your mama's food every day. It would help if you accepted that," she said.

"If you had eaten their food with them, it would have made you more flexible next time, and you wouldn't be a picky eater further down the road. You need to understand that they did their best to cook that food for you," she concluded. Mom feared I would die from starvation when I left the family sphere because I was used to eating her homemade food.

I said, "The food was undesirable; if I had eaten with them, I would have thrown it out."

Before the school year began, on many occasions, Dad would sell one or two sheep or goats to buy school supplies for us. He also sold some of the male goats and sheep to use for family expenses, for health issues, and for purchasing cereal that we could not grow during the previous growing season. He was farsighted.

Most years after the harvest, we had a minimum of two granaries full of ears of millet, small granaries of cobs, and dozens of bags of groundnuts (all kinds), beans, sorghum, fonio, etc. The granaries are rectangular. The walls are hand-shaped with a thin layer of earth that enables the structure to breathe. The roofs are also shaped by hand and covered with straw to protect them from rain.

Dad always proudly said that agriculture played a crucial role in helping him raise all of his children. After harvest, he and Mom would put aside what was needed for home food intake every year and sell the rest of the crop to buy clothes, pay for schooling materials, pay for health fees, etc.

As a pastor then, he was not paid for regular service fees. The tithe and offerings were insufficient to pay a village pastor. He was doing the Lord's work. He and all the pastors in the district obtained a few thousand of local money, francs CFA, once or twice a year. That annual or semestrial payment did not do too much in terms of covering family expenses. Some believers in the community would bring their first fruits/products after harvest to Dad (the pastor) as the Bible asked in Leviticus 23:10. The concept of first fruits is rooted in biblical times when people lived in agrarian society. Harvest time was significant because that was when the farmers' hard work poured into their crops all year began to pay off. They were reaping what they sowed. A man in the village always took advantage of the offering of the first fruits. My parents and all of us children knew the moment and the time. On the first day of his harvest, when he arrived home from the field, he would send someone from his family in the evening when it started getting dark with a basket full of ears of millet. He did the same for maize, sorghum, etc.

Dad was the needle that knitted the community together. He was a teacher, an advisor, and a relationship guru, be it families, friendships, acquaintances, marriages, professionals, etc. Dad also taught literacy to everyone without exception to age, primarily using religious books. But the undisputed legacy he left behind was his contribution to marriages. He rekindled a lot of weddings. As a spiritual leader, he was constantly solicited to bring together falling apart couples on the edge of their marriages. He celebrated hundreds of marriages during his fifty-plus years in the religious ministry and brought hundreds of falling-apart weddings together. When couples come to see him and start accusing each other, he would bring up the first promises they made. First, he would let them know that no divorce is taking place.

Dad would humorously say, "If men behaved after marriage the way they behaved before marriage, half of the divorces would not take place. If women behaved before marriage the way they behaved after marriage, half of the marriages would not take place."

"As a man, is it possible to behave the same after marriage?" I asked.

"Of course, you stay true to yourself. Never have fake behavior or attitude at the beginning of the relationship," he said.

"What about the women?" I inquired.

"Same thing, they need to reflect after marriage what they reflected before marriage," he wrapped up.

For him, a divorce was not and is not an option. You must bring back everyone who attended the wedding ceremony to get a divorce. These people must be present to witness your divorce like they have witnessed the wedding ceremony. Each of them should agree with you two getting divorced the same way they decided to during the wedding. Remember that some of them are no longer, others are traveling far away, and others are sick.

He would remind them of what they had been told on the first day their family began officially. Each of you should play your role and play it to perfection. Marriage relationships never die naturally. It would help if you watched for things that can negatively impact your marriage. They are your attitudes, behaviors, egos, and ignorance. "Ego" especially is a killer. It is only a three-letter word but can quickly destroy a powerful, robust, and twelve-letter word, "relationship." The attitudes, behaviors, and egos will negatively impact and ruin your marriage. He would tell them to remember the commitment.

The moment one commits, there is no independence or freedom from each other anymore. A marriage is almost all about give and take. When both of you are in it for each other, it works. Marriage comes in through the door, and independence goes out of the window. There is no such thing as independence or freedom in a marriage relationship and life. Looking to have absolute freedom is not abiding by one's commitment and is a way of escaping one's duty in a marriage life. It needs to play one's role correctly. You co-depend and interdepend on each other; you fall together, stand up, pick up the pieces, and carry on.

When independence and freedom kick into your marriage, there is no more marriage; it is just a life together in a house. In a marriage, you live in a home. The codependence and interdependence are the pillars of a marriage, and the minor misunderstandings and quarrels are the spices that acclimate the marriage.

Dad's analogy is the following, "remember the tongue and the teeth live together all their life, but the time comes when the tooth hurts the tongue. But they never separate whenever they get in trouble; they pick themselves up, make peace, and live together in complete harmony. They spend more in harmony than in quarrels. This analogy is the same as the situation in a married couple. You are intertwined and have no freedom vis-à-vis the other. True freedom comes from a commitment to a single person who is your significant other and a well-defined purpose together with them. Commitment is the rock that love lives on. Marriage relationship needs engagement, dedication, and connection."

He recommends, "Keep learning and growing better inside every day, keep progressing in your life together, and become a better version of yourself every second. Be a natural person who says what they mean what they say in your everyday communication. Avoid fluff, lies, and pretense. Fast, pray, and meditate together. It helps you to level up your souls as a couple.

As a husband, you have to love your wife, pay for what she needs, provide what she needs, be a good leader, etc. That is being a masculine man, the qualities to have and deserve a submissive woman.

As a wife, you need to be submissive, and submission is accepting the man's leadership. To submit is not to fall back and die down. It does not mean that you are of lower value. You are both valuable equally, but there needs to be a leader. Submission does not take anything away from you being a woman. Expect from your husband things you need and not things you want. Want is never satisfied and will only lead to unrealistic expectations."

We among children used to call him, in our jargon, "Leg," which is a nickname meaning "Daddy," but he was kept confidential to this calling. He passed away on March 11, 2017. At 76. May his soul rest in perfect peace!

My Mom, Esther Kassogue, comes from Indeli, a village a few miles away from my Dad's. She is a typical African queen, average height, dark skin, full breast, and gorgeous. She had long, shiny dark hair. Her hair was so long that she tied it in a ponytail after putting some Shea nut oil and combing it to make it straight. In her youth, she used to be that woman who made you turn around and look again after you walked past her. She is a submissive wife and lets my father lead. Of course, she made suggestions and recommendations regarding decision-making. Often, my Dad asked her for her opinion about an issue, and she would, with goodwill, offer her views. She never raised her voice over Dad. She served Dad with courtesy. She served him food on a tray and regularly asked if he needed anything. She kept Dad's cup for drinking water and coffee apart and separate from others. No one would dare touch what she said with Dad's name on it.

When my elder brothers started working and being productive, they would bring money home, and my Mom always made sure that Dad received the money and decided what to do with it. She was never shy at telling my brothers and me that when we have a gift for our parents, we should give it to Dad first. Her motto was always, "Dad first, Mom second."

She has certainly had the most decisive influence on me. She was full of compassion, love, and kindness. She is a strong, lively, and powerful woman. Once she made up her mind, we knew that trying to change her mind was a waste of time. She is cuddling emotionally as a mother, but she wanted us all to be dynamic and organized in this life. I grew up witnessing my Mom's helping hand. She is always available to help her friends and other people in need, particularly people in poverty. Her concern for needy people is reflected in her everyday life and has never vacated her personality.

Mom loved to play her invaluable role in my developmental stage, as she did for my siblings. She was one hundred percent present in the five stages of a child's development, which are the newborn stage from zero – three months, the infant stage from three – twelve months, the toddler stage from one – three years, the preschool age from three or four years and lastly the school age from four -five, six years. She made sure that we all had the best start in life. My Mom nursed me for as long as she could and showed me her love daily.

I remember perfectly! I was still being breastfed by Mom at age four until five. There was a strange man (in my child's eye) in the village at that time who carried a wooden knife. He had a very long beard and hair. He had never had a haircut, by the look of it. He always met us when I was with Mom somewhere in the village. Whenever he met us, he threatened me to stop sucking at Mom's breast. He vowed I was old enough to be fed from my mother's milk. He would brandish his wooden knife towards me and tell me if the next time he met us, and Mom told him I was still breastfeeding, he would kill me with his knife and gesture his knife in a slit-throat motion. I would scream and tightly hold Mom by her legs and bury my head under her loincloth to not see the strange man wielding his knife. Mom would reassure me that she would not let that happen. She would put both her hands on my back to show her protection. She would tell me not to worry even a little bit because nothing, even a stick, would scratch my head or any other body parts. This man would not stop. He would do and say something every time we met until Dad was transferred to the next village, Pomorododiou, for his pastoral duties a few years later.

I had enough quality food to be healthy and a decent upbringing because my parents were better off financially and better at parenting as time passed. I was lucky to be born later in the birth order, the youngest. As the youngest of the family, I also benefited from the care and kindness of all my siblings. My mother shaped my earlier life. Undoubtedly, the influences and concerns of my parents, especially my mother, motivated me to work hard, get through all the hurdles, and succeed in my studies and professional life.

As the youngest, I always received a particular treatment. But the tolerance zero thing was applied to me as it was for my siblings. Once, Mom sent me to the shopkeeper's to buy something for her. I was ten years old. On my way to the shop, I lost the coin on the sandy street. I tried to recover it, but I couldn't. It was nowhere to be seen. I returned to tell her that I lost the money.

She said, "Let's go! Show me the area where you dropped it?"

I replied, "The street behind our house."

She ordered, "Please take me there."

She had a millet stalk in her hand and was chasing the chickens away from the crushed beans she had spread on a piece of cloth on the floor while I went to the shop. She followed me from behind until we got to where I supposedly lost it. She was using the stalk to make a steering move on the sand.

She asked, "Where exactly did you drop it?"

Not knowing the exact place, I said, "over here."

Before I could realize it, she got close to me and whipped me hard on the back with the stick in her hand. I sped up, wailing to the other side of the road.

She looked at me and said, while pointing her index finger straight at my face, "You will learn the lesson; next time when I send you to the shopkeeper, drop the money!"

Mom talked this way, but I knew it meant to keep the money safe next time and not play around with it and lose it.

Mom is skilled and did income-generating activities such as making bean cakes, crushed ground peas, African locust bean cakes, traditional soaps, etc., to generate income. She did these activities to help Dad out with the household expenses. On market days, Mom would have two big special containers full of bean cakes, dough, Tukuju, etc., which she would take to the marketplace. Some clients were too impatient and could not wait for Mom to enter the market. They would straight come home and buy what and the amount they wanted to buy. Sometimes, Mom would say that these people slowed her down in her preparation to get to the marketplace. We children had our share before Mom left for the market. She would give us the first bean cakes, Tukuju, etc. Sometimes, we would have to wait for Mom to return from the marketplace. When she would return smiling, we knew what that meant for us. It meant that whatever she brought to the market was sold. But when Mom returned, and the container felt heavy, we children would smile because we would enjoy the rest of the cakes. We rarely smiled because Mom sold out most of the time.

Mom is an excellent storyteller, too. She told stories to educate, to have fun, and to deepen the bond between us children. She mostly told us stories full of life lessons. Occasionally, she would talk to us about real-life experiences.

There was a one-eyed young man who was very handsome and tall. He was not born one-eyed. My brothers and I did not know how the attractive young man lost his one eye. One day, Mom told us how he became a one-eyed child. When this young man was a toddler, his Mom was a traditional hairdresser. Women in the village did not have a beauty shop, so they used to plait each other's hair. His Mom used to have women over to her place to plait their hair. She had an iron needle with which she plaited hair. The iron needle let her separate the hair into small, thin chunks while plaiting. One day, her toddler son took the needle to play with it. His Mom took it away from him because it was dangerous for him to play with such an object. When she took it away, the toddler started to cry uncontrollably and wanted it back. His Mom had tried her best to console him, but in vain. She had no choice but to give him back the needle to make him stop crying. As soon as he got it back, he stopped crying, and his Mom was happy he stopped the whining and crying.

A few minutes later, the toddler started screaming and rolling on the floor; when his Mom came over to check on him, he was bleeding badly from his left eye. Looking closely, she realized her son had injured his eye with the needle. When he grew up, his peers were making fun of him, so he asked his Mom how he had lost his eyesight. His Mom told him the story, and her son accused her of being responsible for losing his eye. He told his Mom she could have found another solution to try and stop him from crying. He said he was too young to know what was good for him and what was not. His Mom felt too bad because she failed to handle the situation appropriately.

Mom said, "I tell you this story because I want to let you know that it is a daunting task to be a mother."

"Is it possible to put a new eye?" I asked.

Mom replied, "Unless it is an artificial eye, he can have an artificial eye, but he won't be able to see with it."

"I am sorry for him," I pondered.

Mom insisted, "As a mother, one needs to be present in the child's life as much as possible, at every single step of life until the child is old enough to make a difference between his right and left hand."

"A mother needs to be very vigilant and alert all the time, especially those nursing and tending to babies when they are unable to talk or discern," she added.

Mom said that at this stage, babies only cry when something is wrong; they cannot talk, so they cannot tell you what exactly is going on.

She also told me the story of a careless and unvigilant woman. She had a brand new baby recently and was nursing the baby. In my culture, mothers generally carry their babies on their backs. There are multiple reasons why they do that. Traditional women work hard in the household, and most of their work requires them to kneel or bend down forward. Such activities are washing up, sweeping the floor, washing clothes with bare hands, pounding millet, and cooking food. Because these activities require a lot of bending and kneeling, they carry the babies on their backs. They use a special sheet to tie the baby around their waist and chest. The sheets are specially manufactured for the purpose and have drawings on them. Knitting threads make the pictures.

The drawing area is thick and keeps the baby's poops and urine from sieving.

This woman washed the sheet and hung it on the washing line. When it was dry, she picked it up to carry her baby on her back and went to do some errands. At one point, the baby started to cry and to move his limbs. The mother did her chores while patting the baby on the buttocks to make him fall asleep. This situation continued for a moment, and the baby slowly stopped crying and moving his limbs. When she finally returned home, she untied the baby and looked at him, but he was unresponsive. She first thought he was asleep but later discovered he was lifeless. When they checked his body, they found bruises all over his buttocks and thigh areas. A black scorpion had found its way into the sheet while it was hung to dry. The mother did not realize it when she took it to wrap up the baby with it on her back. During her entire errands, the baby got stung by the black scorpion all over his bottom thigh area and the buttocks. The mother's carelessness and non-vigilance caused her baby to lose his life. She should have shaken the piece of sheet completely when she recovered it from the washing line before tying her baby up on her back. She should have thoroughly checked the sheet for anything that could harm the baby.

Mom said: "you see this? Mothering is a very complex and difficult task".

She insisted, "Only the very vigilant, caring, and tending mothers will be able to be successful in childbearing and child bringing up."

"Staying alert and focused all the time is the state of mind in which a mother should be."

I wanted to know, "Did the baby's mother cry after losing her baby?"

"Of course she did," Mom replied, "Who would not cry?"

"Did the baby boy's father beat her for not paying close attention to the baby's crying?" I inquired.

Mom said, "No." "He was disappointed and could not change what happened."

My Mom was lucky enough to obtain literacy while my father studied pastoral. So, she contributed to the literacy of some women in the village by teaching them how to read and write for free. Dad taught many people how to read and write, and so did Mom. I have seen her spreading and hanging the white and blue sheets on which were written the alphabet letters and the words describing everyday activities. The teaching and writing sessions happened two to three times a week in the afternoon when women finished their household chores. The sessions welcomed the older women and the younger ones alike.

One day, I asked Mom out of curiosity, "Where did the women of the village buy their copybooks?"

Mom said, "They did not buy any copybooks."

"What did they write in/on?" I inquired with surprise.

"On the sandy floor using their fingers," Mom replied.

"How did they learn their lessons?" I asked.

Mom giggled and said, "They only memorized while doing the learning."

"Did they have any homework?" I asked.

Mom laughed out loud, "They only remembered what they memorized and recited the next day during the teaching."

As I was told, one of her most touching and moving life stories was her nursing of a newborn baby. She breastfed babies for different reasons. The first time was when Dad was serving as a trainee pastor in Domounossogou. A breastfeeding woman met Mom and realized she had big breasts with the milk dripping when Mom's baby stopped sucking them. This baby's mama did not have enough milk, and her baby was starving.

She said, "Your baby is full, and you are losing milk. I do not have enough for my baby." So, Mom kindly allowed her to bring her baby a couple of times daily to be nursed.

The second time was when Dad was serving as pastor in Tomotin. A man lived next door with his wife. After his wife delivered, she died from tetanus. During this time, pregnant women gave birth at home with the assistance of traditional midwives.

Mom said, "The midwives probably cut the umbilical cord with a contaminated knife, and it gave tetanus to the poor lady."

The lady died of spasms and stiffness; she had lockjaw, and her spine was arching backward as her back muscles became affected.

The third time was when Dad was serving in Danadoungourou. A Christian woman who lived a couple of yards from our house did not have enough milk for her baby boy. Mom volunteered to breastfeed her baby until she became pregnant with my twin brothers, Jean and Luc. "Did the babies like your milk?" I asked.

Mom laughed, "I have the sweetest milk, and the baby had no choice."

"Was there enough for my brothers, the orphaned baby, and other babies?" I demanded.

"Of course," Mom responded, "I had big breasts full of milk. They were so full it used to drip when I spent some time without nursing the babies."

I asked, "Was it like that when I was a baby?"

Mom said, "I always had big and full breasts while nursing."

I looked at her, impressed and amazed.

She enjoys being valuable and helpful to others. I fondly remember seeing her teach village women how to manufacture local soaps and work along the process of turning cotton into clothes to generate income. During the dry season that starts just after the harvest (let's say between January and mid-June), one of the women's main activities is to work cotton for income-generating activities. Usually, a handful of women in the community used to sit under the nîme tree around Mom to follow the process step by step with her.

Raw cotton is either harvested or bought from cotton farmers and then separated from the seeds manually. This process is demanding and meticulous since each cotton seed is separated from the cotton itself. The following process consists of smoothing out the cotton using a special brush (Yazugole) manufactured for the purpose, followed by the next one of turning the smoothed cotton into threads. The threads are then taken to the weaver to weave them in fine clothes. She is a beacon of hope to most of the people she had crossed paths with, especially the women who were learning the cotton working process.

Mom is a very loving woman as well. She believed in love and stayed faithful to her husband in sickness and health until death. She remained loyal to her vows. That is why she decided not to leave the village for the city even though she was offered the opportunity. She chose to stay in the village because my Daddy passed away in this village and was buried in the family yard (there is no problem to bury someone's body in the family yard). She always says, "The dead are not dead; they are still among us."

So, staying there is one way of honoring Dad's soul.

Of the twelve kids from the Kassogue family, only two are females. All the remaining ten are males. That meant only one thing. Mom had to entrust her sons with some cooking tasks. When Mom was away, especially when she traveled, the kids had to help with household chores—the washing-up, the sweeping, the millet pounding, the millet crushing, and so on. Once, Mom went to the Capital city of the Municipality to buy some condiments and raw vegetables for the family and her incoming generating activities. Before leaving, she had asked the boys to cook beans for dinner.

The boys Josue, Luke, Jean, and Daniel got to work in the late afternoon. They always saw Mom sharing food in a container for Dad, the boys, and the girls. They did not know how Mom measured the amount before cooking. So, they took the container for each group and measured the quantity of the uncooked beans until they reached the usual level when cooked. They gathered all the amounts in the different containers and put them in the cooking pan. As the cooking progressed, the beans swelled until they reached the opening of the pan. They did not know what to do next. Mom arrived from the market simultaneously and found the situation out of hand. She took the biggest of her cooking pan and put all the beans from the smaller pan in it. They spend the rest of the afternoon and evening cooking it. There was food everywhere. Mom had to share it with every family in the neighborhood. When the neighbors heard about it, they laughed and laughed. Whenever these neighbors saw my siblings around us, they joked, "Are you cooking beans today?"

Mom and Dad had their low points, like in any marriage. They had difficult moments and experienced misunderstandings and disagreements, but they never had these moments openly in our presence. They never went to bed showing their angry side openly to each other. Any issue that went wrong between them was solved in their inner room.

As they say, "dirty clothes are washed at home."

Any situation they disagreed on was taken care of in private, alone. They made it their mission not to fight in front of their children. Fighting before their children was never going to make things better.

"Parents fighting before their children would not be able to show good role models to them," Dad said.

My parents talked the talking when they advised us against fighting with each other or anybody else, so they also walked the walking to keep themselves in line with what they expected from us.

My beloved society mainly valued solidarity, hospitality, and mutual care. It has a collectivistic culture. People are very hospitable and always show solidarity and care mutually for each other. Joy and sorrow are shared in the community. One person's problem is everybody's problem, and it is a situation to be taken care of by the community/society. There are always people who care for you; they will willingly help you find a solution. Problems can happen to anyone at any time. Death knocks at anyone's door, and weddings and naming ceremonies are all social events that occur regularly. It is a collectivistic culture through and through. In everything, the good of the people (community) comes first; the interest of the society as a whole matters, not personal interest. In everything, collectivism prevails. Life is very peaceful and consists of sharing the good and the bad bearing each other's burdens.

This is a culture where there is no stranger or foreigner, we are all the same, all equal, and we all matter. When strangers knock at one's door, the first and foremost thing one does for them is to give them water to drink, food to eat, and a place to rest or spend a night or more according to their needs, treat them kindly, make them as comfortable as possible and in particular make them feel at home.

When my father went to be with the Lord, many people came to our house to share our sadness day and night for about a week. I took the long trip from where I was doing my undergraduate studies to attend the funeral of my Dad. I witnessed people offer moral, emotional, financial, and material support. People stayed with us so we would not feel alone and sad.

People consoled us, "Your Dad did his part of the work; now it is your turn to do your part. He was a good man, a truthful, and honest man."

One of the elders insisted, "He was always true to himself."

"The one who stays true to oneself never will disappoint. Go out there and stay true to yourself in whatever you do," another elder said.

Some people stayed with my siblings even for weeks after I left to return to the capital city for my studies. This is how people showed love in helping the bereaved family find solace after their loss. This culture gives a sense to my life; it controls my speech and behavior and determines my identity.

Wedding and naming ceremonies are similar, except that they are happy events and occasions. Among all the happy events I witnessed as a child, one particular event was my elder sister Marie's wedding ceremony. It still sticks fresh in my mind. I was about thirteen years of age but can still narrate in detail my recollection of what the people in the community have done for our family. On the day she was being accompanied to her new husband's village located about fifty kilometers from ours, I remember my Mom's joyful tears as she saw the love people showed our family by offering food and drinks and many other material things such as clothes, shoes, and dishes for the new bride, Marie, to start her new family life with. Even though most people in the society earned a living, they were still able to support and always found ways to help each other financially, materially, etc.

Every child was threatened once or twice about witches while growing up in the village. People sometimes discouraged whining and misbehaving children from acting up by threatening to offer them to the witches who would devour them. I did not like hearing about them and felt sorry that they existed in my society. I entirely rejected them from my culture and hoped they never lived. Witchcraft practice is the plague of my culture. It is passed from mother to daughter and from generation to generation and is practiced mainly by older women. It is believed that their magic power is used for self-defense, and they are expected to use it in such circumstances, but they sometimes use it to harm someone because they do not like, love, or appreciate them.

I was in my first academic year at Teacher Training College in 2009. At the same time, I was a trainee at a Language Center called the Center for Business of Translation and Interpretation (CATI). I was offered the training position by my Linguistics professor at the university, Mister Gueye, who owns the center. I started going there at the end of 2017 and training at the beginning of 2008. I was also in charge of managing the library. The library had two rooms, and I was using one of the rooms as my bedroom. The owner gave me a helping hand so I did not have to rent an apartment. I loved my trainee position by doing a lot of translations (English – French and vice versa). I was also doing well in my studies.

One early morning in April 2009, I received a phone call. The name on the phone screen read Kass Gedeon, my brother who lives in Sevare. It was an unusual time, and it was too early in the morning to receive a call. He never called me that early in the morning. I was asleep, but I quickly picked up as I woke up and said, "Hello," I heard my brother, Jean's voice instead.

He said, "Our Sister Marie has been taken to hospital in Mopti and got an operation on the right side of her neck. She is in hospital as we spoke, and Mom is by her bedside."

Sleep had departed me already. I contacted Mom.

She said, "I was informed a few days ago at the village by a young man on a bike who pedaled the thirty-plus kilometers from where my sister lived with her husband and in-laws."

"On the same day, she was taken to the nearest hospital in the city of Koro, but the doctors at this hospital said it was too serious for them to do anything about it," she added.

She said that is when Marie was taken to a bigger hospital, Hospital Somine Dolo of Mopti.

Mom said, "She is feeling much better after the operation, and I am praying for her quick recovery."

She asked, "Would you pray for her as well?"

I said, "Promised."

Marie's neck swelling was not a natural disease. Her witch mother-in-law poisoned her. Her mother-in-law did not appreciate her son marrying my sister, and my parents were unaware of that at the wedding moment. She also did not understand that her daughter liked and loved my sister so much after the wedding and developed a good relationship with her. Her daughter, even after she got married to a man far away from her family, regularly stayed in touch with my sister as she wanted to show her unequaled love to her.

She visited her family whenever she could, and every time she could see, she spent most of her stay with my sister in her apartment. Everyone in her household and every individual in the village liked and loved my sister. This situation angered the mother-in-law. She poisoned my sister. She lost her life a few days after she received a chirurgical operation on her neck at the Hospital Somine Dolo of Mopti.

After her demise, her husband consulted with my family and decided that her body would not be returned to the village. She was led to rest in Sevare, where she went to be with the Lord. Grave diggers were so surprised when they went to the cemetery to dig her tomb. It was in April, but the ground where she was led to rest was so wet that digging the hole took little effort.

I was distraught in the few weeks that followed her death. I lost my laser-like focus at university and in my training position. Nights were longer, and days were useless and meaningless. I thought of various scenarios and possibilities that could have saved my sister. Was her death avoidable? Was it God's plan? Probably, if she had lived with her husband away from her in-laws in a different town or community.

The Bible says in the book of Genesis, (Genesis 2: 24) that a man shall leave his father and mother after marriage and cleave unto his wife. Both will be one flesh from that point onward. I thought because she lived in the same compound with both her mother and father-in-law, this made her prone and vulnerable to the attack of her mother-in-law. But alas! Too late for that anyway. My sister was gone. I was distraught and heartbroken, and life was so much bitter. It was a nightmare.

I had already planned to visit her during the big holiday just around the corner starting in June. That thought made me feel even worse. I stopped by her village on the big holidays whenever I visited my parents. I always took a long trip to spend a day or two with her, her husband, and their children. A few years back, I visited her and spent two nights there. During the visit, something happened that I only understood after my sister went to be with the Lord. On the day I arrived, in the afternoon, her mother-in-law sent me and a grandchild of hers who was living with them for fresh milk at the Fulani people who lived on the outskirts of the village. The Fulani people kept their cattle outside the village for convenience and accommodation. We returned with the milk a few moments later and took it to her in her living room. We walked past her husband, sitting at the front door leading to their apartment. He was listening to the news on his radio and seemed focused on whatever he was listening to. There, she was sitting on a stool in the living room. She was a short, dark-skinned woman with tiny eyes. She had eye bags, and they seemed like they would fall anytime. We were inside for about a minute before my sister charged into the room, almost running. She looked at me, her mother-in-law, and the milk bottle in my hand.

She ordered, "Leave this living room right away, right now!"

"No problems," I responded.

As I left, she followed me and walked just behind my neck. Once outside, she gestured toward her apartment and said, "Go now."

I went directly to the apartment as she followed me from behind. When we were alone inside her apartment, she took my milk bottle and asked, "Have you eaten or drunk anything from my mother-in-law?"

I shook my head, "meaning no."

She said, "Good!" She warned, don't you ever accept any drink or food from her, Never!"

I shook my head to show my agreement.

She reminded me, "Remember what Mom always used to say when we were growing up." Mom said to never eat or drink from strangers or anybody not from the family. I remembered now why she acted like that. She somehow saved my life. I am a milk lover. My siblings referred to me as the cat because I loved milk as much as a cat, if not more. Mom and my sibling always hid milk from me. My sister's mother-in-law probably knew about it. She saved my life. But she lost hers down the road.

It was in March, and I was lying flat on my back and enjoying the evening breeze. The sky was clear from clouds, and the evening moon was shining as bright as the reflection of a piece of diamond. The stars were scintillating, some of them more prominent than others. I was looking from time to time for a shooting star. I love shooting stars and have enjoyed watching them until they disappear deep into the horizon. I was singing and playing with the cold sand by my mat side. Suddenly, I heard the engine of two big motorbikes riding past our gate. Our door exits to the main road of the village. A few moments later, I heard a familiar voice saying tie her up and take her away. Screaming from a young lady followed that. I focused, cleared my ear, and listened again carefully. It was Sama's voice. I sat down then and realized something serious was happening in the neighborhood.

I asked Mom, "Do you know what is happening? Do you recognize the screaming voice?"

She said, "It is Sama's wedding, this is her voice. Mom said she is being taken to her husband's village, about fifteen kilometers away from our village," Mom said.

I said, "I did not hear about it."

Mom responded, "It is a forced marriage. They always keep it a secret so the bride does not find out and flee."

I was frightened; deep down, I felt this was unfair and even criminal. I said, "Sama is a very nice girl who never harmed anyone or did anything wrong. She is living her life, is innocent, and does not deserve this," I lamented, "this is the worst thing that can happen to a woman."

Mom said, "It is the culture, even if not common now, most young people are denied the decision of a partner choice and when they can get married."

She added, "Parents unconditionally expect their children to marry mates of their choosing." "Refusing to comply with parents' choices means being cursed," She said, "The one who refuses shows disrespect to parents and has to leave or will be forced to leave their parental home because they are no longer considered a member of the family in many cases."

Mom stopped for a while and gathered her recollection, "There are various reasons behind arranged or forced marriages. Most of the time, it depends on promises made by parents at birth. Most parents promise to give their daughters or sons through marriage bonds to their friends and acquaintances' children or even their relatives' children."

She regretted, "Generally, when children grow up, it turns out to be not their cup of tea. Sometimes it works out, but frequently it does not."

Mom paused and said, "Some young people reluctantly accept, but others categorically refuse and commit suicide instead. Some others flee on the night of the wedding ceremony and would not be heard of until after a long time or after they have gotten married themselves to a stranger."

That forced or arranged marriage I witnessed as an adolescent still sticks in my mind. It was the first time that I had seen the entire village in a state of complete sadness. A young girl who refused to marry a man her father chose was tied up and taken to a remote village on a sad night. She was screaming at the top of her voice and asking village people to come to her rescue and prevent these people from taking her away to a man she did not love. But nobody came to her rescue since it is cultural; people understood it to be expected. I bet people, every single person in the village that night felt something. I had no doubt everybody heard her screaming as the riders rode through the village street. I was lying down while listening to her screaming until it dwindled. And the saddest of all these is that the relationship did not last long. They divorced a few years later when I was in high school and went their separate ways. I did not know about the ex-husband, but Sama married another man of her choice.

Danadoungourou, the village where I was born and spent my tender childhood, was peaceful, hospitable, and had a harmonious, close-knit community. The village numbered a couple of thousands, most at the time. My family home was separated from the church by a road on the outskirts. During the dry season, from the inside of our compound, which was fenced with millet stalks tied up with sliced animal skin ropes to dry tree branches, I could see the multiple roads that connected the village to other villages and towns from inside the compound. I could see the well, the common property and good, where women drew water for their daily needs and where cattle breeders and shepherds watered their animals after pastures. I could also see the farmlands, which lay empty as far as the eyes could see that were used for farming during the rainy season. I enjoyed the sight of women drawing water from the wells as early as six o'clock in the morning. There was no tap or running water, so the water from the wells was used for drinking, cooking, washing, etc., serving the entire village. The scenery of women, some with babies on the back, drawing water while talking to each other, was so beautiful. These women mostly wore a traditional cloth called "Soï Gara = dyed fabric." It was the typical standard attire for the women of the era. Soï Gara was dyed dark blue after the white fabric was sewn with hand needles (hand-woven). After dying, the sewn parts are detached to reveal the drawings. The drawings on the cloth vary from stars to half-moons to drops of water. The women wore this cloth from head to toe (headscarves, shirts, loincloths). Men also wore it but with different types of styles. Their outfits were hats, long-sleeved shirts, and pants. It was not as standard attire for men as for women.

Women of the village were involved in some income-generating activities, such as the cotton transformation into the fabric used to make the "Soï Gara." Women buy the raw cotton from the local market to work step by step to obtain the fabric. The step-by-step process occurs during the day after women finish household chores such as fetching water, cooking lunch, laundering, etc. Usually, small groups of women, four to five, gather at someone's house to work raw cotton while they talk about everything and nothing and enjoy their time together.

During the dry season, older men used to sit at the Toguna. Toguna is a kind of thatch structure mainly known as a space for pastime, peace, conflict resolution (social justice cases), parties, and social events. Usually, senior people, the semi-retired or retired from "farm" work, the early retired (have enough children grown up to take of them), those too old to work, or those physically unfit gather there to share daily news, discuss their upbringing of the young of their community, change their environment, air and relax away from the family sphere. Toguna is where elders gauge the present and future well-being of the community in general. From the Toguna, elders have both the bird's eye view (they are high up in terms of experience) and worm's eye view (they hold together the community) of the society, and that would allow them to examine it thoroughly.

It is also where elders test children to see whether they will be good citizens, wise souls, competent beings, and well-rounded citizens who will reach their full potential. A child is known by his/her deeds, whether their work is pure or right or wrong. For instance, elders call some passing by young children over and give them some valuable items, and then one of the elders would ask the young child to present or share the valuable item with him. If the child accepts the request to share what he/she has just received, he/she is deemed kind and generous. If the child refuses to share after receiving the gift, he/she is considered mean and wicked. In the same vein, some elders would send children to get something from the vendor or get an item from their household and bring it to them.

A child who complies with the request is rewarded, and the one who refuses is considered disrespectful towards the elders and will not receive blessings from the elders. A compliant child's reward can be some dried meat from a wild animal taken out of the skin bag of a hunter or some coins that he or she can use to buy some Tomujo or Tukujou (snacks such as bean cakes or peanut-based products).

To a good child in attitude and behavior, elders will say: "In Souls Nobly Born, Valor Does Not depend Upon Age." To an evil child, they will say: "Your buttocks are there for spanking and your back for flogging."

Occasionally, justice is served at the Toguna for members of the community who are in conflict (in such cases, men and women participate in the process). The elders are the judges (the wise of the village). Grey hair was synonymous with wisdom then. A famous saying goes, "The hair of the elders has not turned grey for nothing." It is through life experiences and hardships.

I witnessed an unfortunate conflict resolution case during a call between two young men from different neighborhoods who fought over an issue. The issue was that one young man's donkey ate up the crops of the other young man at the farm while they both were busy with farm work. The two had beaten each other up in the field, and one was seriously injured. The jury was held in the late afternoon, and all the spokespeople from each neighborhood were present. Many people (men, women, and children) from the other communities were eyewitnesses and earwitnesses.

The eldest (the wisest) of the elder, Baelu, took the floor and enumerated the bylaws of the Wagu. The "Wagu" is a god by which you take an oath and solemnly affirm you to tell the truth. If it appears that one party is telling untruths, that party will lose their life. The two had to take turns putting their hands on the Wagu and take an oath to tell exactly how things unfolded. Baelu was known as the chief of the hunters and one of the best hunters of his era. In his prime, he used to hunt down all kinds of wild animals, and he had the skins of all the animals he had killed in his mystic room (man chambers). He owned the black powder firearm for hunting and demonstration during festivals and parties in the village. As one may know, in the villages, traditional feasts are organized to celebrate the harvest and other happy occasions. These traditional feasts showed hunters their know-how in handling black powder firearms.

During these festivities, hunters were rated and praised according to the loudness of the sound of their firearms when they pulled the trigger after loading it with the black powder. Anybody familiar with these types of weapons knows that the black powder does not tolerate water. It needs to be kept dry and away from moisture and humidity. When wet, it will not ignite the weapon. But Baelu was a man of a thousand tricks; he managed to ace where others would fail miserably. He used to load his firearm with black powder, fill the barrel with water, and pour out the water before pulling the trigger. His gun was heard in all the neighboring villages and beyond. The sound of his firearms is even known by people who lived in those neighboring villages. His body was moisturized through Shea butter, but his facial skin had wrinkled, and he had eye bags due to old age. His lips were discolored with cola nuts and traditional snuff (powdered tobacco). His teeth were decayed due to the smoking of his bent pipe that he always carried with him.

He was a man of great mysteries, well respected in the village, and famous for his charisma, uprightness, transparency, and integrity. He held the record of being the most impartial judge in the village's history. He topped his father, grandfather, and even his great-grandfathers. He was so thirsty for justice that he got nicknamed the "undisputed." That is because people tried to bribe him on many occasions, but in vain, so great was his integrity and fairness. He was small in stature but big in personality and character. He was in his eighties, but he was very clear-headed. He was considered the greatest of all time in terms of generosity.

He used to say: "God, do not grant me anything if I cannot share it with others. We live together, we laugh together, we mourn together, we party together, we die together, etc."

After he was done with the rules of the "Wagu," the floor was given to the donkey's owner to narrate his story. He painfully stood up (because of the injury he was carrying) and respectfully greeted the elders for giving him the floor and started to detail how he had tied the donkey down with a leash in a hereby bush to work on the farm. He insisted that he did not intend to let his donkey loose so it could eat up the crops of one of his loved ones. He lamented that he was sorry for the damage caused, but the education he received from his parents would not allow him to do such a shameful thing. He admitted that he would be sad and angry at the same time if his crops were eaten up.

In his turn, the owner of the crops stood up and addressed the elders by saluting them and commending their commitment to settling the case. He persuasively accused the donkey owner of tying down his donkey too close to his crops, and the donkey, tempted by the taste of the crops, broke the leash to free itself. He added that this was not the first time he tied the animal too close to his crops and that he had witnesses who could testify.

"That is not true!" retorted the owner of the donkey. "I...

"Stop it!" Baelu shakingly (annoyed by the interruption made by the owner of the donkey) stood up and ordered the owner of the donkey to sit down and stop talking, "You do not do that here. Have you forgotten the rules that I just stated. When you had the floor to speak nobody here interrupted you. Isn't that right? Now, sit down and let him finish". "You do that again, you will be heavily fined for breaking the rules. If he is lying, the "Wagu" will take care of him." "A word to a wise is enough!"

"Continue, please..." he said.

Apagna responded that he was finished giving his side of the story. He wanted to ensure that his witnesses could confirm that when necessary.

Baelu cleared his throat and thanked the two men for explaining the situation. He also thanked the audience for listening silently and with great interest.

"Now, let's see, you both are not wicked. You both are under my watch, and I can confidently say you have clean sheets for making trouble in this village. Your record is blameless until now. I know that you, Apagna, did not tie your donkey so it could get loose and eat up some of the Aperou's crop, and you, Aperou, I know that anger did make you act that way. Now, we will find a middle way to solve this problem. Each one of you will be fined according to the breach you made. Apagna, you will apologize to Aperou and pay back the quantity of crop your donkey eats. Aperou, you will pay for the full treatment of Apagna's injuries." He pronounced.

Baelu then addressed the public and hollered: "Do you agree with all these proceedings?" And the crowd responded, "That is a fair judgment." All the young people started shouting: "Long live Baelu! Long live Baelu! Long live Baelu!"

Some of the adults and younger men of the village were seen busy fetching firewood for the household, taking care of the domestic animals, going hunting, or working the Banco using husks to make bricks for constructing houses, fences, barns, huts, etc. In contrast, other men were busy transforming the Banco into mud used for plastering previously built houses, huts, fences, etc. This is one of the activities that men performed that caught my attention. The process of transforming the Banco into strengthened mud is exceptional. The Banco is mixed with millet husk, cow dung, or animal droppings to strengthen mud. The strengthened mud covers the various buildings to protect them from Mother Nature. All the buildings in the village are made of Banco bricks, and the plastering of these buildings with strengthened mud is necessary to prevent rain from washing away the houses, huts, fences, etc.

The community was dominated by framers sprinkled with shopkeepers, merchants, cattle raisers, and animal feeders. Some women feed animals, generating income. They do these animal-feeding activities with their left hand in addition to being homemakers. Also, a few families of blacksmiths lived in the community. They were at the service of the framers, who needed them to manufacture tools necessary for agricultural and other gardening-related activities. Only a few activities were going on that could spoil the air and the environment. I enjoyed life in the village, especially during the rainy season. Rain is enjoyed differently by people of all ages. I want rain because when it rains, I am fond of raindrops hitting the roofs of houses and the ground. I used to play in the shower and jump in the puddles. Rain clears the sky from dust, and everything is clean and sounds fresh. My Mom is very good at making bean cakes, and on rainy days, my siblings and I were happy to gather around her and enjoy the fresh bean cakes from the frying pan.

The rainy season comes around the first week of June, the time of the year when natural beauty comes into existence. When the first rain hits the ground, grasses sprout from the land. I could see the green scenery inside our house in a few days. I used to walk in the grass barefoot and felt the freshness of the grass and the rustling noise it made under my feet. Sometimes, when it rains, I wake early the following day before the sun has risen and the dew has evaporated to run around to get my feet soaked. I used to run by keeping my feet near the height of the grasses so my feet touch the top of the grass.

The rainy season is the busiest moment of the year. It is the growing season. During this season, men rise early to go to the farm to grow crops. One could overhear as early as five in the morning men's voices exchanging usual greetings. Sometimes, one could hear voices of men passing by as far as a few hundred yards, asking about the well-being of each other's family members and the progress of the growing season on their way to the farm. Greetings take a long time in the Dogon culture. It can take five to ten minutes. Greeters will ask about the well-being of each other, their spouses, grandparents, children, nephews, cousins, nieces, grandchildren, and great-grandchildren for minutes on end. It is like the first one who stops asking will lose something. So, they would continue until their voices died down, and they could not hear each other anymore. Sometimes, one feels that some people are done with the greetings. They would be talking about regular activities and come back to ask about someone they did not mention in the greetings cycle. One feels the love people express in their way of greeting.

The main activity is agriculture, and the main crop is millet. Besides millet, sorghum, maize, beans, fonio cereal, peanut, etc. are also grown. Women who participate less in the growing activities stay behind in the house. They first fetch water from the well and cook food to bring it to the men to the farm later in the morning. Women then help men in the growing work during the day, but they stop work early enough to make it home to get ready, shower water for men, return home in the evening, and fix dinner for the family. This process lasts two to three months, enough time for the ears to develop and ripen. When the crops are picked between September and December, they feed the family for the dry and rainy seasons, which run from October to June/July to September the following year.

I went to school at the age of seven years in Pomorododiou, a village in the fifth region of Mopti. It is a peaceful village. There were a lot of ethnic groups. The village was divided into six small neighborhoods. Dad was transferred from Danadougourou when serving as pastor at the local church. When I started school, I was under my parents' watch. The school I attended had only six classrooms from first to sixth grade—two blocks of buildings with three classrooms each. The buildings were semi-hard. They were first built with mud bricks and coated with cement mixed with sand and gravel. The inside floor of the classroom was plastered with cement mixed with fine sand, and worked with a toothed trowel to make a uniformed surface. The yard of the entire school was covered with grass in October every year when school started. The school's principal would take a day off every year during the first week of school to clean the yard and get rid of the grass.

Most of the school's teachers were transferred from remote locations throughout the country. We heard of them only after they had traveled and settled into the village. I was registered in school with most of my neighborhood's kids. Kids from the neighboring villages also attended school with us because no schools were there. They walked the two, three, and four kilometers to attend school all day and returned in the afternoon. They carried their bottles containing millet cream and water, plastic bags containing crushed millet, crushed ground peas, etc.

On the first day, while walking to school with my hand in Dad's and my school bag dangling down from my left shoulder, a man who used to tease me all the time saw us and walked up to us to talk to us.

He said, "From this day on, you will not be able to accompany your mother everywhere in the village." He insisted, "From this time onwards, you will be busy with homework and school duties."

Dad agreed, "It will indeed be the case."

He continued his way after saying those words. I only listened; I did not say a word. I was so anxious going to school, my mind wandering, my heart beating hard, and a cold sweat running down my forehead. I was convinced I would feel alone without anybody from my family around me. As soon as we arrived at school, Dad greeted the teachers and exchanged a few words with some of the already there teachers. One of the teachers, who was wearing spectacles, spoke with me. His glasses were too old that they were smoked up.

He asked, "How old are you, son?"

"Seven", I said.

He then asked, "What is your name?"

"Benjamin," I answered with a shaking voice.

He told me, "Go to one of the rooms in the first set of classrooms and enter the first-grade classroom." I anxiously, silently, and slowly walked towards the building while Dad and the teachers looked at me and talked. I looked back a couple of times before I reached the entrance. I entered the room and found many kids in my neighborhood seated on the cemented floor. The room was quiet, and most first graders felt anxious, just like me.

When we generally met in the community, we played together, but on that day, we wore a different face. We were anxious. We were told that if we refused to study well, we would get beaten, spanked, slapped, our ears pinched or pulled, etc. We each carried a cloth bag with a slate, chalk, pencils, and a double-line thin copybook. I sat in the front area with some of the kids from my neighborhood. The teacher, Mister Aboudou, walked into the room moments later. He was a light-skinned man with mixed white and dark hair and beard. He was the oldest of all the teachers and the school's principal. He was a nomad and came straight from the northern part of the country, where all nomadic people originated.

As soon as he entered, he asked us to leave the classroom and stand in line before the entrance. He made us stand in two lines and taught us some steps that we would take every morning from that day to get into the classroom. All the pupils would listen to the teacher say the following and gesture at his order.

He would say: "On tend, Fixe, Repos, Attention... One, Two - One, Two, ready? Go!"

After a few rehearsals in front of the classroom door, the teacher would order us to get into the classroom. The pupils would start walking at the rhythm, get into the classroom, and be seated. Once in the classroom, he sang the national anthem and told us we would be taught as the year wore on. He also said we would be required to sing the anthem every morning when raising the flag.

In the first week of school, the teacher showed up in the classroom carrying a few textbooks in his hands. We numbered about forty-five in the classroom. He split us into groups of five and six and told us that one of us would be responsible for keeping the book on behalf of the group. The teacher asked each group to designate someone.

When the teacher reached my group, he asked, "Who wants to take care of the textbook in your group?"

I quickly responded, "I will keep the textbook on behalf of the group."

Unfortunately, everybody in my group also wanted custody of the textbook. We all wanted to have the textbook and make the most of it, but we needed help. Finally, the teacher decided that everyone in the group would have the textbook for a couple of days and in turns.

There was a young man who was super intelligent in my class. This young man's dad and my Dad knew each other very well. They always took time every night to exchange words after the evening prayer at the church before bidding goodbye to each other. This guy was undisputed and topped us in almost all major and optional subjects in school. Whenever we had a test in subjects such as reading, calculus, writing, etc., he always came top in all the subjects, even in some secondary subjects such as dictation, course questions, civic education, etc. The teacher tagged him. I used to cry every time I failed to match him. My Dad never minded me not being at the top of the class.

He praised me for good grades and said, "I am satisfied with your performance and effort."

I showed him a happy face and smiled every time he said so.

Mom also encouraged me in her ways, "God will nurse his children in turns, the way a mother nurses her baby from the right or left-hand side to the other."

She would insist, "A time will come when you will be top of the class."

This boy continued to outwit us one way or the other until we finished primary school. I was undefeated in the writing of the different letters of the alphabet. I always had the top grade. I was the calligrapher in third and fourth grade, and even in middle school, I excelled.

We went to another, more extensive town in middle school because our village did not have a middle school. The intelligent boy and I were separated for convenience reasons. We were in the same town but in different middle schools. I at least had peace of mind because I did not have to compete with this geek. I stayed with my oldest brother, Josue, the family's first-born son, serving as a pastor in the town. I only studied there for one year.

I returned to my Dad's village when the village had a middle school the following year, and I completed my middle school there. My middle school years were great. There were only three classrooms, and it was located a couple of yards from our house. The principal, Mister Traore Lassine, became a friend of my Dad in the year he arrived, and I befriended his firstborn Sidiki and younger brother, Adama. Both of them were in the same middle school as me. During the academic year, we played soccer together. During the big holidays, we generally played cards together while making green tea from China, and we had numerous beautiful moments of our adolescenthood together. One night during the big holiday of 1999 – 2000, we played cards as usual, but things went too far. We were making too much noise late at night, which blew the principal to his top. He was trying to sleep, and the endless noises prevented him from falling asleep. Usually, he did not have any problems with us playing cards late into the night, but this night was different.

He came out of his door with his sleeping clothes and shouted at us, "You guys, stop the noise! Who do you think you are making that much noise this late into the night?" "Go play your cards at Benjamin's parents' house and make the noises there!"

We were too much into playing cards that night, and we did not notice either the noise we were making, which was too loud, or the time passing too late into the night. We packed up our business, put the cards down, gathered the tea material and the table we used for playing cards, and called quit for the night.

We played soccer three times a day--early morning before class, between the school break time during the day, and the evening after afternoon class. There was a playground between the local health care center building and the middle school building where we played soccer. The playground was used for cultivating peanuts during the rainy seasons. There were thorny trees on the four sides of the playground. One of the trees, called cailcedrat, was very tall and bore many fruits. This giant tree was just around the corner of the playground. It interfered with our soccer practice because it occupied most of our playing space. It got rid of its spiky leaves and thorns from October every year until February or March. It made it harder for us to practice soccer because most of us played bare feet and could not run or walk near the cailcedrat tree with thorns and spiky leaves. I was one of the few who had shoes on while playing soccer. I had an old All-Star that I used to play soccer with. When I got past the ball, I would run with it towards the cailcedrat tree, deterring the bare-foot guys from running after me to recover it. It annoyed most of them, but they did not have any choice.

They had to buy shoes to play with if they were mad at me. I always used the route "cailcedrat" to run with the ball towards the other team's net to score goals. The principal's brother, Adama Traore, a good dribbler and an excellent ball passer, and I were always on the same team. He was the one who always passed the ball to me. He was playing with shoes, too. So, he would pass the ball to me a million times, especially if we were not winning the game and were a goal or two down.

Playing three times a day entertained us so much. We enjoyed playing, but our parents, who lived close to each other, were concerned about us playing in the sun at noon, especially during the hot season from March until the end of May. They feared for our health and decided to approach the principal and ask him to prevent us from playing football during the midday break on the school playing field. The principal summoned us one day to his office after evening class and told us that from that day, he wanted to see us clutching our copybooks and textbooks rather than playing football in the sun.

When not playing football or cards, we would tell jokes in turns. Sometimes, we told real stories; other times, we made stories to make each other laugh and enjoy our time together. One of the famous real stories we repeatedly laughed about was a story told by my friend Adama. He is a dark-skinned, short young man. He told the story most hilariously. It was the story of a Bamanan (ethnic group in Mali) man and a Fulani (ethnic group in Mali) man. They both were involved in a theft. They each stole a bull in a neighborhood and were caught red-handed. So, the leaders in the community decided that one of them would be castrated and the other would be killed the following day. They were both locked up. In the middle of the night, the Fulani man called some of his people into his cell, and they concocted a plan. They planned to convince the leaders in the neighborhood to castrate their thief brother before morning. This way, they could save him from being killed. They did everything they could to convince the leaders to castrate their brother, who was castrated before the following day.

The next and only penalty is the killing, which was the destiny of the Bamanan man. When the time of the punishment came, all the men of the village gathered to witness the situation. Nobody in the village knew about the castration except the Fulani and the neighborhood leaders. Meanwhile, the notable of the village called an emergency meeting overnight to solve the situation without murder being committed and blood being shed, so they decided to meet the neighborhood leaders and beg them to reconsider their decision. The notable approached the neighborhood leaders and prayed to them, and the leaders accepted. The leaders freed both the Bamanan man unscathed and the Fulani man with tears running down his cheeks in front of everybody.

I would ask, "What did the Fulani people say?"

"Nothing, they were ashamed," he would reply.

I would ask, "Was the Fulani thief able to walk home?"

He would respond, "Nope, he was on his knees crawling, he could not stand up, his stomach was aching as hell."

That made every one of us laugh uncontrollably. Some of us would say, "The Fulani people thought they were the smartest people, but they were the dumbest of all."

Middle school years were fun, and I had good grades in most subjects and was comfortable in my studies. But something was outstanding about me, and that was my skills in drawing maps and writing beautifully. I was famous for being the best map drawer and the calligrapher of the entire middle school in ninth grade. It spread fast when the school principal who taught us literature, geography, history, and grammar wrote these words on my geography copybook: "Best cartographer, best calligrapher, graded "Excellent."

The principal later explained that the maps (of Africa, Mali, etc.) I have drawn in my geography copybook were as beautiful as the writing I have done in all my copybooks in his subjects.

I left Dad and Mom to travel about two hundred kilometers to attend high school. I attended Lycée Hammadoun Dicko de Sévaré. Sévaré is about twelve kilometers from Mopti, the capital city of the fifth region. I lived with one of my brothers, Gédéon, the small business manager of SFI. (*Sécretariat – Formation – Informatique*). During my three-year stay with him, I got familiar with Computer Science (Word – Excel – PowerPoint, etc.). My high school endeavors were as smooth as possible. I did not perform as well as in middle school, but I did just fine.

The atmosphere was good, and the environment was friendly. Many kinds of people were in the high school and among the teachers. However, there was a confident, fearsome man in this high school. In every school, there is that ugly figure that many students are scared of, and many dislike so much. In my high school, there was one genuinely terrifying man. This man was the high school's supervisor and the bogeyman in the entire high school. No student messed up with the code of conduct and the rules when he was around. The bogeyman would get you if you were terrible, did not abide by the rules, and would make you pay for it. He was very strict about wearing the school uniform, being a one-off, and showing a polite attitude in the compound. He never condoned misbehavior and allowed no student to make mischief around the school. He was that shadowy, amorphous ghost who hid in the corners of classroom rows to catch his victims. He was almost invisible and walked unexpectedly towards unsuspecting victims to punish them.

He always had a whip or two dangling from his right shoulder and flogged the guilty ones with his lashes, which hiss as viperous tongues over them. For the lazy, unfocused, and undisciplined students, he was an ugly, gaunt man who kidnapped and maltreated them in broad daylight. He brought a lot of discipline and stability to the school.

Some teachers impressed me with their mastery of their subjects; first, my English teacher, Mister Batolo. He was nicknamed Bartolo because he resembled a telecast character that was so popular back in my high school days. He was a short, dark-skinned man in his fifties and loved teaching English. I could not wait for him to get into the classroom, and I always completed my assignments and homework on time and proactively participated in class. He delves into the fact that English is the lingua franca of the world; that it is the language of opportunities, and people admire you when you speak English, and they right away impressed by you.

My French teacher, General Ousmane Doumbia, was a poet in the making. He pushed us to punch above our weight in our learning and practicing of artwork and emulating the poets and writers whose work we were studying in class. In twelfth grade, during one of the tests, General Ousmane Doumbia was so impressed by the result of one of my assignments that he read my entire assignment to the classroom. He praised me for doing an excellent job. We read and studied poems from Victor Hugo, Honore de Balzac, Baudelaire, whose famous quote, "The finest trick of the devil is to persuade you that he does not exist," Voltaire, who said, "Judge a man by his questions rather than by his answers," Jean Paul le Sartre, whose unforgettable quote "Man is condemned to be free; because once thrown into the world, he is responsible for everything he does," set me on my path.

And finally, our philosophy teacher, Mister Kisso Djiga. He built us up through the famous Greek philosophers. Through the Socrates method, he instilled in us a yearning for knowledge, and through Palto's philosophy of education, education is a means to achieve individual and social justice. We learned that the well-being of society and harmony in our community depend on knowledge of one's job, self-knowledge, and the idea of good. Social justice can be achieved when all social classes, workers, warriors, and rules are in a harmonious relationship. There is no peace without justice! So, I have learned.

Upon graduating from high school, I moved to Bamako, the capital city of Mali, to study at university and lived with my brother Jean. Jean was in the final year of his studies at a teachers' training college.

Bamako has an entirely different environment, too. It is foggy, dusty, and dirty. More than in the villages and towns I lived previously. Bamako was as crowded as a beehive, and going places was difficult. One had to walk between buses, cars, motorbikes, and wheelbarrow pullers to get to places where one wanted to be. I used to walk to places in the village and the region, but in Bamako, you must do more than just that all the time. Areas were located far away from each other. The most common public transportation was the buses or the Sotramas, and you had to wait for them somewhere and be on their timetable. There were also taxis, but not everyone could afford them. I was so freaked out whenever I had to go downtown or to university.

I felt very uncomfortable using public transportation. There were many kinds of people using them, and I was sometimes ill at ease inside those public transportation buses. The inside of the buses was dirty, and the conductors' assistants were friendly when you met them at the bus stop, but they would suddenly become impolite once you got on the Sotramas and paid the fare. The Sotramas are packed inside, and the conductors' assistants do not care if you are well seated. And after you pay the fare, you have to fight tooth and nail to get your change back. You would have asked them for it nonstop; if not, they would pretend to have forgotten. Sometimes, I used the Sotramas, but other times, I just walked the distance no matter how far away it was. I used to cross the Martyr Bridge (860 meters) and King Fahd Bridge (0.97 kilometers) on foot a few times to get registered for classes and take classes. The university is located on the hill of the Badalabougou neighborhood on the city's right bank, divided by the Fleuve Djoliba or Niger River. I lived on the left bank.

After registering for classes and before the beginning of courses, I traveled with my brother Jean and some tourists, Danish architecture students, to the Bandiagara and Mopti regions. These tourists came to Mali to learn from its architecture. The tourists spoke Danish and English. They needed help understanding French or any other local languages spoken in Mali. My brother Jean and I served as interpreters for them. We took them to Dogon land, Banani, and Sangha in the Bandiagara region for two weeks so they could explore and learn from the Dogon architecture.

We then took them to Djene, in the Mopti region, for two more weeks to gain more insights from the particularity of its architectural buildings. In Djene, I met a man while working with the students in architecture. The man was chosen by the leader of tourist guides of Djene to give some specific information about the architecture of Djene city, where all buildings were made of mud, even floor buildings. Building houses with cement and sophisticated materials inside the city was forbidden. Anybody who wanted to build in cement had to do it outside the city.

This man was well known in and outside the city for his knowledge of the city's architecture, housing, and planning history. He was an average man with dark skin and a round belly. He was so damn hairy, and felt proud of it. He incessantly stroked the hair along his arms, beards, and sideburns. I had to translate his accounts into English for the Danish student architects. They gathered around him and listened religiously to him while I was translating. The students were impressed by him for his knowledge about the city and its architecture. He was impressed by me and my translating job.

When we finished, he asked me, "How old are you, and where did you go to school?"

I told him, "I am x years old and a freshman at university. I graduated from high school a few months ago and am a newly registered student at the University of Bamako."

He could not believe his eyes and ears. He said, "At this age and level of study, you did very well in translating. In a Francophone country like Mali, people had to travel abroad to learn the English language effectively."

He added, "It is impressive, and you are doing an awesome job even without traveling to an English-speaking country to learn the language."

I said, "Thank you for your encouragement and compliment."

When I returned to Bamako, classes had already started at university, and two weeks had been completed. My brother bought me a motorbike, Dragon Sanili, with the money I made doing the consecutive interpretation. I was happy about purchasing the motorbike, but life was still difficult because money was scanty. My brother used my motorbike many times, though he had his own car. I had to take public transportation (the Sotramas) to university. I had to take the Sotrama twice to get to the university, but I preferred to take it only once to get to Rail Da, a public transportation hub. From there, I walked to my university.

On the days I had classes, I went to the university and spent the entire day there. During the break, my classmates would ask me to follow them to the Deguedrome. Deguedrome is on the other side of the university building, where a woman sells millet cream mixed with milk. Most students from the university would buy Degue (the millet cream) from her. She was very famous, and her Degue was very delicious.

They would always invite me, "Aren't you coming with us for lunch, Benj?" I always found an alibi to stay in the classroom. After they would have left I stayed in the classroom to read from my notes or read one of the booklets I bought from some of my professors. My classmates always went to Deguedrome to have some Degue for lunch.

Most of the time, I told them, "I am not hungry."

They would always ask even though they knew my answer was always the same, negative. The problem was that I needed more money to buy lunch, the booklets, and the hand-outs we used in the courses from the professors. So, I purchased the booklets and hand-outs and spent the day with an empty stomach.

I was fending for myself most years of my undergraduate studies except for a few months. I stayed with my elder brother Jean, who was finishing his second training as a high school teacher as a freshman. We lived in a neighborhood away from downtown, where the rent cost of the apartment was lower. We rented a two-piece apartment, one bedroom, and a living room located inside a big house belonging to the Maraka (an ethnic group in Mali) people. The house owner was insane and was very difficult to get along with. His parents, wife, children, and other relatives lived in the big building with the lessees. He was a very tall and handsome man with a dark complexion. It was hurtful that such a wonderful man had an unsound mind. He was a very successful international trader, but he suddenly became mad.

The rumors around his situation were that someone put an evil eye on him. A jealous person attacked him mystically because of his successes in business and trading. This attack resulted in him being a madman. He always had a ring of beads and used to sit in the sun in the neighborhood, sweating and counting the beads. While he was sitting and counting the beads, his older daughter would sometimes bring a wet towel and put it on his head to protect him a little bit from the sun. They repeatedly tried and begged him to get inside, but he never agreed to do so. He sometimes walked more than six kilometers to the Grand Mosque downtown to pray for a few minutes and return home.

We could not watch TV or listen to our radios at the average audible volume when he was around the house. He hated these things. When he was home, and we started watching TV in our apartment, his wife would knock at our door to plead for us to turn down the volume before her husband would realize it. Most days, we would turn on our TV, turn the volume down, and sit as close as possible to hear the news. His health was sporadic. He was off and on. It looked like someone was turning the screws behind the scene to make him feel bad or worse. When he was recovering and feeling better after receiving treatment, the person would turn the screws to turn his mental health terrible. That was when he turned everything on his way upside down. Rarely was he sound and talked with people usually, sat down with his wife and children, accompanied his daughters to school, and played with his baby boy in front of his house entrance. He even came to see me a couple of times so I could help him write the receipt for the payment made by the lessees and make him sign under the lessor's name. He was being treated and was taken now and then to the healer somewhere in the city.

One day, in April 2006, my help was solicited to take him to a healer somewhere in the city in a van. He was tall physically and very strong, and a few gentlemen were needed to restrain him. He hated being taken to the healer, and his old mother sometimes begged him to accept being brought there, but in vain. The last option was to take him there against his will. We had to force him to get into the van that day. We managed to take him to the healer's place, and I had to wait outside for them. I stayed out for about thirty minutes while they dealt with the healer. I have no idea what happened inside when they came out, but he was quieter, calmer, and stable. One of his relatives was carrying a black plastic bag with dried leaves. He kept it so careful and did not want other people to touch it or offer to carry it for him. Driving home was less eventful than when we were driving out there.

When we got home, his people heated the dried leaves with water to get a potion. They summoned the young men in the neighborhood, including me, inside a room to restrain him physically, give him a shower using the potion from the dried leaves, and give him some to drink. We had the potion in a bucket and took it inside the inner room, where we had him undressed. He took two mouthfuls of the potion and refused to have any more. His relatives were happy he had the two mouthfuls. Next was to bathe him. We had him seated. I had both my knees on his legs while he was sitting to prevent him from moving.

He said, "You idiot, you will break my legs with your weight."

I relaxed a little bit to give him some pause. I asked him after lifting one leg, "Are you comfortable?"

Instead of answering, he pushed me away and used his leg to knock down the bucket. The entire potion spilled all over the floor of the inner room, right to the very dregs. I was disappointed, and so were his relatives. I did not know how much they had paid for this medication, but it was all gone. I stood up with my head in both hands. I immediately recalled one of our discussions in high school while in twelfth grade with our philosophy teacher. One day, he asked us what we thought was the most severe disease in this world. He gave us a few days to think about it and said we would discuss it during next week's class. Before the next lesson, we did a lot of homework and confidently came to class. Some of us said it was HIV AIDS, others believed it was leper, others said cancer, blindness, and the list went on and on.

The professor listened carefully, looked at us, and said we were all in the same ballpark as most students he taught. Most people believe so, but he said the most severe disease is losing reasoning. When someone loses reason, they are useless and live two lives: a first sane life and a second insane one. In the second insane life, they most often do not know what they want and what is good for them. When someone has no reason, that person gets naked before everybody's eyes, goes to the toilet in front of everybody, eats rotten food, etc.

This man's people were doing their best to bring him healing, which I did not believe could heal him, but they tried anyway. They prepared an expensive potion to help him, but he ruined it.

Growing up, I feared mad people randomly coming to our village. Mom said I was right to be scared of them because they could harm or kill me badly. This man's situation reminded me of one of my mother's life experiences. She believes madness is indeed the most severe disease, and it is based on what she lived to see in this world.

Mom witnessed an unfortunate situation when traveling in a neighborhood village on a market day as a teenager. Hallway through to the village, they saw a young man selling meat by the roadside. A few people traveling in either direction of the road had stopped and stood a few distances from the young man. The young man was mad, and people were surprised where he had the meat and why he was trying to sell it at this hour of the day between two villages in the bush. He was inviting the people standing around to come to buy his meat. Some people who knew the madman were surprised to see him alone because he was often seen everywhere with his Dad, who took him on the back of his donkey to healers in the area so he could get treatment.

On this day, the donkey stood tied up at a tree and he sat under the tree before the meat. It was later discovered that this madman had killed his dad while taking him to a healer in a remote village to be treated. He had killed him, cut his body into pieces, put the pieces into piles, and tried to sell his dad's body to travelers, bystanders, and passers-by.

Madness is just sad. This man seemed so innocent. I felt for him, but at the same time, I had to focus on my studies because the academic year was closing soon.

Towards the end of the academic year, when we were having the final exams, which were planned over an entire week, I had an accident while traveling to school with my motorbike. My brother Jean, with whom I was staying, had traveled to the village and left the bike with me. So, I bought fuel with the bit of money he gave me to meet my needs before he returned from his trip. It was the last day, and I would sit for the few remaining subjects at the end of the school year. The accident happened on the main road leading to the Grand Marche de Bamako. An older man with his Yamaha bike cut in front of me. I tried to avoid him, but I could not. I hit him, he fell right there, and I fell a few feet ahead and slid about ten meters away on the asphalted road.

A motorist was behind us, avoiding running over the older man and running into a lamppost instead. Someone was yelling at me to stay put. This someone was adamant I should stay lying down on the floor. But I stood up and ran at the older man lying flat on his back. I looked at his face and could only see the whites of his eyes. I was so anxious, panicked, and freaked out. The back of my right hand was white due to the scratching on the asphalted road, and the right side of my head was white from scratching the asphalt. Soon, both my hand and head started to bleed. Firefighters were called immediately, and they quickly arrived on the scene. They laid the older man on a stretcher and put him in the back of their vehicle.

One of the firefighters walked up to me and asked, "Please follow me and get in the vehicle."

I said, "No, I have an exam, and I need to get to university as quickly as possible to sit for the exam."

The firefighter looked thoughtfully at me and said, "You are about to die and refuse to be taken to hospital."

I told him, "I survived hunger for eight to nine months. These little injuries from the accident would not kill me. I would have died from hunger during these last eight months if God wanted my death."

He looked at me, shook his head in amazement, and left to join the others in the ambulance.

An acquaintance, a young man who used to visit his friends in my neighborhood, ran into me at the accident scene. He was a young trader at the Grand Marche and was going there early in the morning as usual.

He asked, "Are you sure you are not going to hospital?"

I reassured him, "No, I have an exam and I really need to go to the university right now."

He said, "Fine then; if you are not going to the hospital and want to go to the university, I will give you a ride there."

I accepted, and he dropped me off at my university. Upon arriving there, I quickly hurried into the public toilet to wash the wounds on my head and hand and went to sit in the classroom. A classmate offered me some cream, an ointment that I applied to my head and hand. During the exams, the supervisor saw traces of blood on my head and hand and noticed that I applied some creams.

He asked, "Did you have an accident?"

I confirmed, "Unfortunately, I was on my way here when I crashed into an old man who cut in front of me with his bike."

He did not say anything anymore but realized my commitment and dedication to take the exams anyway.

After the exams, in the afternoon, I asked a female classmate to give me a ride to where I generally take the Sotrama, but she gave me money to ride the Sotrama instead. I kindly refused her money and decided to walk the kilometers I usually walked to ride the Sotrama. From there, I rode the bus to my brother Enoc's apartment to inform him of what happened. He is a photographer and a tailor and does his best to make both ends meet.

He asked, "Where is your motorbike?"

I said, "I left it at the accident scene."

He said, "So, let's go recover the motorbike."

We went there and asked the agents, and they told us that the police took the motorbike to the sixth police station. We went there but were told to go to the twelfth police station instead because the area where the accident happened was under the surveillance of the twelfth police station. We went there and found the vehicle's owner and the son of the older man I hit waiting for me there. The policeman listened to my account and put it into the record book. I was sent to the chief of the police office with my brother accompanying me.

When I entered, he asked, "Where are the papers of the motorbike?"

I only had one, the purchase paper. I did not pay road tax and had no insurance.

The policeman took my ID card and said, "Young man, you would be punished for not paying the road tax and not having insurance."

He added, "You need to pay approximately six thousand Francs CFA, ten dollars."

I put my hands in my pocket and took out some coins amounting to two hundred and twenty-five francs CFA, about forty-five cents. I handed out, "Here is the whole amount I have for myself." I added, "Since the accident, I have not eaten yet."

The policeman looked at me and had a feeling for me. He told me, "Go to see the owner of the car and the old man's son and agree on something, and then come back to see me."

After exchanging a few words, the owner said the insurance company was repairing his car and that he was fine. He just wanted to finish with all these and go home. The older man's son also said that his Dad was feeling better and he had nothing against me or the vehicle owner. I also said I have nothing against any of them. So the police officers freed us, and my brother took my motorbike from the dozens of stolen and accident cases motorbikes. The motorbike was partially damaged. While riding to his apartment with me, he stopped at a drugstore to buy some permanganate. When we arrived at his place, he shaved the hair on the injured part of my head and used the permanganate to dress the wounds on the head and the hand.

Despite the struggles and the unfortunate accidents, I excelled in my exams and validated all the subjects. I did not even go to check the results. One of my classmates, a young lady named Penda, gave me the news. Panda is an easy-going, always smiling, open-hearted, easy to get along with, and cheerful girl. She is very eloquent and befriended everyone in the class.

She texted, "Congratulations on validating all the subjects in the exams!"

I texted back, "Thank you so much! Are you on the campus, right?"

She replied, "I am right here looking at the results."

"What are your results?" I asked.

She responded, "I failed in three subjects, so I need to retake them to validate the year."

"Good luck, Penda!" I wished.

I expected nothing less. I always thought I would validate every subject. After hearing the news from Penda, I felt emotional. She touched my soul. She failed to validate some of the subjects, but she felt so happy for me for validating all subjects and went even further to send a text message to congratulate me. A friend of mine who had also failed to validate some of the subjects felt the same when I showed him the text message from Penda. She is lovely and shows what kind of a human being she always is.

I also lived with a widow, Mrs. Traore, who welcomed me into her house for about seven months as a sophomore. She is one of those rare mothers available to help everyone in need the way she possibly could. She had no problems sharing what she had and shared it with passion and happiness. Only sharing what she made her feel valued, glad, and valuable. She lived with her five children, three sons and two daughters. She did not mind welcoming me into her house after my brother Jean had graduated from teachers' training college, returned to the town, and joined his family. She gladly offered to accommodate me and treated me on equal footing with her children. She provided me with a single room about three meters square. It was spacious enough only to fit my motorbike, my suitcase, and my single-place mattress in it. I only put the bike inside at night when I went to bed. The room was supposed to be a store room of the apartment. But I did not mind. I loved it. She gave me the same love, care, and openness as her children.

She even gave me money to buy clothes. After I returned from downtown one day, she came to my door and called me by my name.

"Benjamin?" she called out.

"Yes, Mah," I responded and came to the door of my room.

She held out an amount of ten thousand francs CFA. "Use this money to buy some clothes."

"I have money to buy clothes, Mah," I said. "You are helping a lot by accommodating me." "Please, take this. You did not ask for it," she insisted, "I gave it to you from the bottom of my heart."

I had no choice but to take the money, "Thank you, and God bless you."

This woman arose early every morning at five before anyone else and woke up her children so they could pray the Fajr prayer together. "Cham, Abo, Bub wake up. It is time to pray," she would call out every morning at five for Fajr prayer. After the Fajr prayer, her children went back to sleep, and she stayed awake and fixed breakfast and put it on a platform meant for us when we woke up to go to school.

We always woke up to find breakfast ready, and she was nowhere to be seen around the breakfast table. She was gritty and relentless. She reminded me of my Mom, who was always there for people in need and would never mind helping out with a smile, food, advice, etc.

While living with her, I worked part-time in a nursery by planting seeds, watering, tending plants, and selling plants. I worked there every day of the week except on Sundays during the holidays. I would go to the nursery early in the morning and stay there all day to return home in the evening. During the school year, I did this job with my left hand as I had to go to university to take classes on some days. On the days I had classes, I stayed in school all day and did not go to the nursery. The rest of the week, I would go there. The owner of the nursery, Mister Paul, is a tall, dark-skinned man. He is well-built and lean. His nursery activity contributed to his better health.

He said, "When one sits inside the nursery, they are protected from the road dust because the leaves of the different plants will aspire the dust;" he also highlighted, "the temperature gets milder as from the plants on the edge of the nursery."

"Why is that so?" I asked.

"It is because of the watering of the plants, which keeps humidity around." he confidently responded.

One of my professors who inspired me at university is Mister Coulibaly. He is originally from the Segou region, which is the fourth region of Mali. I was privileged to be his student for two years (as a freshman and a sophomore). He taught general and special translation as well as conversation. During these two years, he touched my life through his character, attitude, and self-respect. He was my professor and later he became my advisor and some kind of a mentor and now I befriended him. We are perfect friends. In my first two years at university, I noticed that he was a one-off person; he still is. He is very punctual. He came in on time and left on time. He was very well organized.

When he was unavailable for class, he would inform us ahead of time (one or two weeks before). When he promised something, he delivered. He was a genuine Bamanan person (an ethnic group in Mali known for their uprightness and integrity). He showed integrity, honesty, and purity in his everyday behavior. His self-respect was incredible. He did not do the wrong thing in the wrong place or time. He was also a great communicator. His life skills were there to be seen by everyone. On a few occasions, he welcomed me into his home to help with my translation exercises. During the exercise sessions, he offered me pieces of advice on life. I also called him occasionally to get advice for any severe decisions I was making until I completed my undergraduate studies.

A Baby by the waste dumps. Bamako is a city where the unexpected occurred. You wake up one day and see something you have never imagined to see or experience and live with it for the rest of your life.

I witnessed a situation that hit me to the core. One morning in winter, I was sitting with some guys from the neighborhood in front of the translation business office I worked for. It was very cold, and we were enjoying the early sun rays. A lady, Bahawa, was used to frying millet cake on the other end of the street. We saw a young man, a tall one, with a baby in his arms, a baby dressed well in pajamas, and a hand-knit bonnet for babies to protect him against the cold. He walked past us without greeting and continued down the street. The street he walked into was less practical because there was no open exit, and it was a no-go zone because during the night, crimes were committed there, drug dealers had their deals there, and people who unknowingly walked on this no-go street at nighttime were the victim of violence and robbed of their possessions. The lady, Bahawa, sat on the road's edge and followed his movements and actions.

She was looking at him and wondering, "Where on earth was he going with a baby early in the morning in a dangerous street such as this one."

She stopped frying for some time and followed the young man seated at her frying space. When the young man reached the big waste dumps at the end of the street, he put the baby there, walked across the pond, and disappeared into the woods. Bahawa quickly ran there and found the innocent baby sitting comfortably at the foot of the waste dump. She took the baby and brought the baby to the family house facing my office building. She told us that the young man who just walked by had put the baby by the garbage pile and disappeared into the woods.

We all rushed into the compound to see the baby. The baby was very handsome, with dark and complete hair. The baby was looking at each person standing there. He was only seeing new faces all around. When I looked at the face of the baby, I had goosebumps all over my body. A lady in the family undressed the baby, and we all discovered at the same time baby boy. I was shattered, tears running down my cheeks.

I said deep down, "As long as you are alive in this world, you will see things." I could not believe my eyes.

I was shaking; it was cruel, and the culprit did this in cold blood.

"While some people are paying money to have babies, others are getting rid of them in the saddest ways," I said.

"You are right," answered one of the ladies in the house.

The police were called in to take care of the matter at hand. The police drove the pickup vehicle to the waste dumps, but the young man was nowhere to be found. A lady, a civil servant, lived in the neighborhood. She failed to carry a baby in her marriage, and her husband had already passed. She wanted to adopt the baby boy, but the police said they could not meet her request on the spot. They took the baby boy to foster care services. I spent the next several months affected by this act. Every time I thought about the whole situation, the face of the baby appeared to me.

While studying at the university, I wanted to continue my studies after obtaining an undergraduate degree. I registered at the American Cultural Center at the US embassy in Bamako to exploit the library and be abreast of scholarship opportunities. I was reading everything readable that had fallen into my hands. I read about fifty to sixty pages of books on the internet, newspapers, and Newsweek from the embassy library. In addition, I checked out books from the American Cultural Center for fifteen days. I was researching every lead out there to know more about the US education system to supplement what I studied at the university. I approached anybody with any knowledge about the American education system, like the alumni, the professors, the peace-corps volunteers, etc.

After graduating from Teachers' Training College, I started working all day every day except Sundays at the languages CATI (Center for the

Business in Translation and Interpretation). My boss, Mister Gueye, was physically small but mentally and intellectually a baobab, a giant. He used to play football when he was younger. He was a hardworking man who impacted his students and everyone he crossed paths with. He is undoubtedly the best I have known in teaching English as a foreign language, conducting translation and interpreting from English to French, and vice versa. I heard about his reputation even before I registered for his classes. He taught linguistics and bilingualism. He has the best-ever tricks in teaching idioms, proverbs, and slang, and he is comfortable at it as much as a spider is comfortable at creating its webs.

He wrote a French-English translation booklet in which proverbs, idioms, and slang were translated into the target language, and short, complex texts were also translated. I was so impressed with him. He is so good at what he does that I jokingly said deep down to myself that if only I could get twenty or thirty percent of his knowledge, I would be fine. He was so good. When he started interpreting simultaneously, one would say the words, expressions, and speeches were coming from a radio or some automated machine manufactured for that purpose. I spent more time with him on translation tasks. I was part of a team of translators, and when we were done with translating, we would put together all the translated versions, and I would take the one file document to him so he could proofread and harmonize the work. When we did the translation individually, we would translate using our terminologies and words we had deemed accurate and faithful to the original. He would comb through the entire document regarding terminologies, words, and expressions and meticulously refine it to meet the client's wishes. I was always there for the proofreading tasks, and we did it together all the time.

He also loved doing it with me because I am tech-savvy, and he was happy to let me control the computer. I would open the documents (French and English versions) on the computer screen. I would sit in front of the computer screen, and he would sit just behind me or by my side. When we started proofreading, we would go word for word, sentence for sentence, etc. I was uncomfortable and excited at the same time. Uncomfortable because no mistakes and errors we made while translating would escape his vigilance. He would find out that we did not know some translation basics, which made me uncomfortable. I was excited because it was always a learning opportunity every time we proofread together. While proofreading, errors, mistakes, and mistranslations caught his eyes the way a magnet caught pieces of iron. He would say this was not the right word, this was not the appropriate sentence, and this was not the faithful translation.

He would keep pointing to the mistakes here and there until we finished the whole document and it was ready to be sent. When we were proofreading, He used to say that they were spanked in school when they made mistakes while learning the language skills. That's why they could do those language tricks better than we would.

After we sat through proofreading many pages, he would say, "Benj, I will not get old and have my back with me. My back will be gone by the time I will be in my seventies or eighties."

That meant his back was paining him for sitting down so long. I would encourage him, "You will be fine, and do not worry a bit."

Next, we would attach the document in an email and the invoice to send to the client. He would always write in the email to whoever was the client to expedite the payment of the invoice. The funniest part was when we sent the translated version to the client, and I mentioned it was sent. He never trusted the computer when it displayed "sent."

He would ask, "Open the sent messages section and let me see the attachment on the message we just sent."

I would respond, "Yes, it is sent, it says."

At the end, he would say "You already know", Benj, "I never trusted your computers or your internet or your whatever. I was born when "Mali" was called "Soudan Mali." I cannot trust your machine one hundred percent."

He would say, "You guys are the Coca Cola generation; you are more intelligent than us regarding computers and new technologies."

He insisted, "There will be no guarantee it has been sent until I checked and double-checked, and it has been confirmed that it has been sent indeed."

Later, when the payment was ready, he would call me to get the check or cash. One afternoon, when we were proofreading, he received a call from one of our faithful clients to collect the money for some translation we had done a few days ago; I said I would get the money when we finished the proofreading.

He said, "No, let me counsel you, Benj, never do that again. When you are called to be paid, stop everything you are doing right away and go get the money first," he insisted on that, "In this life never put off being paid, besides for a job already completed."

While working with this man in his language center, I kept applying for the Fulbright scholarship every year. He is a former Fulbrighter who excelled in his studies at Buffalo University in New York and holds a PhD in Linguistics. He even wrote letters of recommendation for me every time I needed any scholarships I applied for.

I applied, I failed, I applied again, I failed. I applied over and over again until I was successful in it.

On one occasion, I applied and successfully passed the interview step; I spent a lot of time preparing for the test. A glitch in the testing room had the applicants waiting a long time on the test day. At one point, it was decided that the trial could not be done anymore. We were asked to leave, and the Educational Testing Service would reschedule the test for another day. As promised, I received an email confirming my rescheduling on another date. I was happy and hoped that the trial would run smoothly for the good of all of us on the next occasion.

On the test day, I woke up as early as possible, took a shower, and took my bike to ride to the center, where the test did not occur the last time because of a technical error. When I got there, there was nobody there yet. So I parked my motorbike and sat on top of it. I took out my HP computer and started doing some last-minute practice. The test was supposed to begin at ten o'clock but we, the candidates, were told to be at the center at the latest thirty minutes before the starting time. I was there before nine o'clock, so I was fine in terms of time. I sat there until nine-thirty, and nobody showed up, not even the administrator. I wondered why nobody was there thirty minutes before the test was supposed to start. A few minutes later, I saw the test administrator, Mister Sanogo. I felt he was surprised to see me there.

He asked, "What are you doing here?"

I responded, "I am here to take the TOEFL test."

He shrieked, "The test is not here for today. It is at the other TOEFL center."

The test center he is talking about is about ten kilometers from there.

He said, "Please go there quickly because the test starts at eight-thirty at this center, and it has already started."

I jumped on my bike and sped up there. All the applicants were already in the middle of the test. The administrator of the iBT TOEFL test there, Mister Fofana, was angry with me for being that late.

He inquired, "What happened? Why you are so late?"

I said, "I did not know the test was here, I..."

"Please, stop." He cut in.

He said, "I really doubt if it will still be possible for you to take the test with the others, but I will try to have you take it."

He was able to do so, but I was in panic mode and could not concentrate as much as I wanted. When I was in the reading section, the other candidates were doing the speaking and writing paragraphs, and that made focusing very hard for me. Everybody else was talking. So, I botched the test! I missed the first visa, and everything from there was down and bottom.

The last time I applied successfully, I prayed about it and let it go. The first line of my application reads like this: "The United is the leading country in the field of education, technology, science, literature, agriculture, etc." My ambition to go there to study is to obtain a master's in education to contribute to the development of my country upon my return.

One day, in June 2014, I was on consecutive interpretation duty at a conference on a power improvement project between Mali – Ghana – Burkina – Cote d'Ivoire at the headquarters of a national structure located next to the Pyramid de Souvenirs. I received a call with a nonregistered number, at first I could not pick up the call because I was in the middle of interpretation.

I later called the number back during lunch break, and the person at the other end said, "Hello, Tim speaking. Are you Benjamin?"

I responded, "Yes, It is".

He said, "I am calling to tell you that you are invited to an interview for the scholarship you applied for."

"Thank you so much for calling," I said.

"Please be in our office, at the US Embassy, on Thursday at ten o'clock local time"

I said, "I will be there". I shortened my interpretation duty to prepare for the interview. Meanwhile, I called some former people who obtained the scholarship to give me some pointers.

On the interview day, I arrived half an hour earlier and stood at the US embassy's front desk. I did my best to be in the right mindset. I had a thorough preparation, and I felt prepared and confident. I broke some sweat when I saw the escort meet me at the front desk. We walked into the interview room, and there were seven people. It felt like they armed themselves to the teeth, ready to bombard me with tough questions.

The first interviewer asked, "Could you speak about your background?" I detailed the answer.

Another interviewer asked, "Why do you want to study in the United States?"

It was the most welcome question because I already knew the reasons why. I praised the country as the best in many fields, particularly education.

The following person asked, "Could you define curriculum since you plan to study in this field?"

I felt comfortable answering this question as well.

Another interviewer asked, "What could you bring to the US from this country."

I responded this way, "I wanted to bring respect to old age, I always thought that young Americans did not offer senior people the respect they deserved."

The interview chair thanked me for my time and said they would get back to me if my interview were successful and I got preselected for the next step. I thanked them as well for taking the time to review my application and having me at the interview stage. One of them escorted me out of the room and to the front desk and bid me goodbye. I said I was looking forward to hearing from them soon.

I went home and got down with my work head down. Exactly a week later, I received another call that I was preselected for the next step: taking the iBT TOEFL test. I was already prepared for having practiced the test material for the last ten to twelve months. I knew I would not botch or fail this time because this could be my last chance ever. A few weeks later, I took the test and scored higher than expected. However, I had to wait seven long months to have confirmation that I had been offered the scholarship I had wanted for the last four to five years.

On January 21, 2015, I received a phone call from Mister Mariko, the Cultural Affairs Specialist at the Embassy, around eleven in the morning. He is a man who has his heart in his hand. A very handsome man from the inside out. A truthful, honest, upright, and sincere man. He worked at the US Embassy for over thirty years and was trusted and respected by all on the embassy premises, men and women alike. Over the years, he guided, counseled, and advised hundreds of Fulbright applicants and helped them obtain the scholarship. He did not care about the applicant's physical stature, ethnic group, or skin color; he only cared about their ability to pursue higher studies and whether they deserved the scholarship.

He phoned, "Hello! Ben, this is Mister Mariko."

His first question was, "Where are you, Ben?"

"I am at the office," I answered.

I worked as an English teacher, a translator, and the assistant to the Chief Executive Officer.

He said okay, "I am calling to inform you that you are offered full funding for the scholarship you applied for."

I was thrilled, "Really? Thank you, God, Wholeheartedly!"

"Congratulations! You deserve it, Ben." He said proudly, "You will be revealed later the name of the university you will attend and the date of the upcoming trip. Thank you."

I thanked him for giving me some of the best news I have ever received. Next, I got on my knees to thank God Almighty wholeheartedly. I thanked him for assisting me throughout the entire process. I remembered that, over the last year, I had sung songs to pray for him. One song I regularly sang was "Danaba An ka Ala Deli Ala Na An Aka Deleli Jabi". It is a Bamanankan song from the songbook "Betiba." It means, "Believers, Let's Pray; God Will Answer Our Prayers."

I informed my Mom first and then my brothers and sisters. My Mom told me to pay her a visit to the village before going on such a trip.

CHAPTER 2

A Trip Like No Other

On the evening of my trip to the United States of America, a gentleman I knew very well named Yougo, who is of the Maraka ethnic group, offered to give me a ride to the airport in his brand new Range Rover Evoque shipped from the factory. I had planned to hail a cab and whizz to the airport. When Yougo offered the ride, that plan was put aside. Yougo, like most young men of the Maraka ethnic group, was a successful businessman in the Grand Marche de Bamako.

The information I had about Yougo was that he owned a stationery store and a sizeable Bazin boutique. Bazin is a delicate garment from Dubai. The Maraka people only cared a little about attending school or doing long studies. They cared more about doing business and anything related to it, like start-ups. They started doing business at a very young age. Children from this ethnic either did not attend school or dropped out after a couple of years to start small income-generating activities such as shining shoes, mending wearing out shoes, polishing nails, selling handmade clothes, etc. This ethnic group always lived in extended families where a man had two to four wives and a dozen children. When the children grow up, they marry and stay in the family, extending it. Their families were so big that there were up to twenty to fifty in a single one. The more children one has, the wealthier one is.

In addition, their children make a financial contribution by doing small and odd jobs. Children aged as low as seven from these families involved in income-generating activities were required to contribute financially to the family's expenses. These children leave the family sphere early in the morning with a small backpack containing their shoe-shining brushes, nail polishers, etc. They return home in the evening after spending the entire day working downtown, making money.

Before leaving the house the following day, they would drop a coin or two in a box reserved for purchasing condiments and groceries. Yougo also went through the same process to become a successful businessman he is today. He is so successful nowadays and lives a comfortable life. He is part of the group of people who were called the yuppies (young urban professionals). These are young, affluent, and successful business-wise men, and it is apparent in their lifestyles and possessions. When Yougo heard that I was traveling overseas for higher studies, he could not believe his ears. He was impressed by what I had achieved in terms of studies.

Even though Yougo was a wealthy businessman, he did not have any education to allow him to fill out a form or write a check. He was even more impressed when I told him that I got a fully paid scholarship with air tickets, health insurance, and accommodation for the entire stay included. He had stopped and parked his Range Rover Evoque by the roadside on his way home from the Grand Marche de Bamako. He was seated with another friend in the same business as him. He had waited until my departure to the airport so they could return home together after dropping me off. His Range Rover was a dark satin and copper styling touches outside fitted with an18-inch diamond-effect aluminum alloy wheels and LED headlights, which left the passerby in awe. The inside had a reversing camera, rear parking sensors, and a 10-inch touchscreen infotainment system featuring DAB radio, Bluetooth, sat-nav, Apple Car Play, and Android Auto. The seats are made of perforated leather and are very comfortable. The ride to the airport was as comfortable as one could have imagined.

My flight took off on Tuesday, September 15, 2015, at 10:45 pm local time for a twenty-eight hours journey (unplanned) with a layover in France at Paris Degaule. I took off from Paris Degaule around nine o'clock local time to fly to Atlanta and landed there sometime in the middle of the day. I did not check the time because my legs had already started feeling tired. A million people from around the world were in line for customs services. I saw people from different backgrounds with backpacks and carry-on luggage clutching their passports. Some were very impatient waiting in line. Some passengers were also called over to a small room for random checking. I stayed in line for about one hour before receiving the customs services. I had barely finished with customs services when it was time for my next flight. I quickly got my suitcase to register.

Before I got to the registration desk, a police officer stopped me and asked if I had anything dangerous in my suitcase. I said I did not have anything of such nature. I told him I had my clothes and some traditional soaps my Mom had made for me to use in the US. He then ordered me to open my suitcase. I did so, and he checked it out and let me go. I hastily registered my suitcase and sped up to the terminals. When I arrived at the gate, the plane had already left with my suitcase.

I went to the front desk at the airport to explain the situation. The lady behind the desk took my itinerary and boarding pass. She looked at it for a while and made some phone calls. She then asked me to be patient. I stood there waiting for her to solve the issue. I was constantly thinking about my host Mom, who had planned to pick me up at their airport according to my itinerary. A few minutes later, the lady at the front desk issued a new boarding pass. While leaving, she said something I could not understand because I was hurrying up to board the plane. I begged her pardon, and she made some gestures while talking. She meant I should not stop, start looking around, and miss this plane too. I almost told her I missed the layover because the airport workers, especially the customs agents, were very slow in checking. Since I wanted to save time, I kept going. I was able to board the flight to fly to San Diego.

From there, I called my host Mom to inform her of my delayed arrival. She said no problem. She was already at her daughter's house in downtown Portland and would stay there until I arrived. I boarded another plane to get to Portland. I landed in Portland at about ten thirty at night (maybe), and my suitcase was waiting for me on a table close to the pickup area. I called my host Mom from one of the phones of the airport workers at the reception desk. I have called her from these people's phones since I set foot on the American territory to let her know my whereabouts. She already had my itinerary but was in the dark with me missing my plane in Atlanta. She showed up some twenty minutes later with her daughter Bessie at the wheel of her Chevrolet to pick me up.

She saw me standing at the pickup area and recognized me from far away. As soon as they pulled up, she said: "Ben?" This is first of the million times she called me that way.

I said, "Yes". She signaled and said, "Please put your suitcase in the trunk and get quickly in the car. We need to drive away and free the space for others coming to pick up or drop off their people." I did so and got into the car.

She jokingly said, "You described yourself as wearing a pink jacket, but it is brown."

I jokingly said, "You are right," "I had a long trip and was not recognizing the colors anymore."

We all laughed at that little misunderstanding. It was a typical autumn night in Portland. I sat in the back of the car, studying both my host Mom and her daughter. It was like we were driving through Disneyland. The vivid colors of the streets leading to the airport were very pleasing to my eyes. My mind was racing with different thoughts. This was my second trip to the USA (another state), but everything seemed new. It is a new state, people, culture, environment, food; how would I cope with all that? I will live with a single-parent American family and cannot afford the luxury of not liking a particular food.

I was taken to her daughter Bessie's home, and she was my first host in downtown Portland. She offered, "Could I bring your suitcase upstairs to your room?"

I kindly declined the offer, "I can do it, thank you anyway."

As a true African gentleman, I could not let her carry it upstairs. Deep down, I told myself you had already done enough by picking me up at the airport late into the night and offering to welcome me into your house, a stranger.

Bessie is a very tall and robust, typical African-American girl with curly hair, dark skin, and a little bit overweight. She could carry the suitcase into her grandson's room, which would be my room for the next few days. Even late into the night, she had some dinner ready for me. She probably knew that I did not have food during the in-state flight. While I had the quick dinner, she sat on the couch and waited for me to finish. That was so sweet of her. After dinner, I went to bed straight and slept for ten hours nonstop. I felt so tired and so jet-lagged that I felt numb.

The following day, I was told that Harris, Bessie's grandson, was waiting to see me even though he never met me before. He was a curious, bright, and handsome child. This is the first time for him to meet someone from Africa face to face. He heard about my coming and was looking forward to meeting me on my arrival on the same day, but alas, the trip took a long. He waited in vain and went to bed with his Mom, Bessie's daughter, who was also a single Mom, so I was told the next day after I had woken up and met him. I later learned that he gave up his room to sleep with her grandma during my stay so I could feel comfortable and have privacy. What a wonderful, hospitable, loving, and caring young man! I told him it was nice of him to allow me to have his room for my short stay and that I appreciated it.

The next day, at night, my host, Bessie, called me downstairs to watch the film "Coming to America" with her friend, Barb, her daughter Alexis, the mother of Harris, and Harris himself. It was an act of welcoming and allowing me to feel at home. It was my first time hearing about the film, but what? I did enjoy it. Anybody who has heard about or seen this film knows the quality and the more profound message it sends out. This movie is about a prince who went on an adventure to find true love. The film's hilarious part was when the prince said, "I attend the University of the United States." I burst out laughing, and the rest looked at me with a sense of surprise. They were glad that I liked the characters and understood their English.

On the second day, I went to open a bank account at United Bank on North East Shaver. My host Mom recommended that I open an account there. From there, I went to the market with her to buy a new phone at Verizon. I had to inform my Mom, who had been praying for my safe arrival back home, that I reached my destination safely. My Mom was in an area where Internet connection was nonexistent. So, the only way to contact her was to make an international call. I bought a calling card from Pingo to call her and all my siblings to give them the news of my arrival in the country of Uncle Sam. Some of my siblings were living in different places throughout the country. They were all happy that I had a safe trip. I also had to inform some friends I was living within my community in the capital city about my arrival.

After a few days at Bessie's house, my host Mom came to pick me up and drove me down to her house in North East Shaver Street. She had already taken me to her home to visit and get familiar with the neighborhood. She showed me around the house and my unavailable room during the visit. I moved into her house after a few days at Bessie's. It was evening time, around dinner time. The neighborhood was tranquil, peaceful, and conducive to living. Her house was spotless, with rugs all over the floor. The walls of the house were covered with scriptures and motivational messages. The most noticeable for me was the prayer of Jabez verse. A mighty devotion from *Jabez to God, "Oh that You would bless me indeed, and enlarge my territory, that Your hand would be with me, and that You would keep me from evil, that I may not cause pain!" So, God granted him what he requested. Chronicles 4: 10.* While looking at the scripture, I was wearing my flip-flops and did not realize that everyone had taken their shoes off and left them at the entrance. The rule of the house was to leave your shoes before stepping in.

When she noticed it, she could not believe it and asked: "Are you wearing shoes in my house, Ben?"

"Oh, I am sorry," I apologized straight away.

Even though she knew that I did not do that on purpose, she expected me to know it. I quickly apologized and returned to the entrance to take them off. She had already cooked a special dinner, orange chicken, one of my favorite foods in the United States. She set the table up very neatly and nicely. It looked delicious and healthy and brought saliva into the mouth just by looking at it. I was hungry and wanted so much food that I got some pieces before the dinner started. She pushed off my hand and ordered me to wash my hands.

Food was always available at my host Mom's house. She would ask us, me and Vincent, to list what we wanted to eat for the next couple of weeks before shopping, "Write it down for me, please. I cannot remember all this." She repeatedly told us to eat food. She always said it would go wrong if we did not eat. She begged us not to make her waste her money. Mom always made sure we had enough food to eat. She had two refrigerators, one in the kitchen and the other in the garage. They both were always full of all kinds of food.

She repeatedly urged us, "I want you guys to eat; there is food in the refrigerator. I bought them for you guys," and, "Let me know if you need anything." Mom never missed an occasion to highlight the importance of staying hydrated. She would always remind Vincent and I to drink water,

"You need to stay hydrated. Please drink eight glasses every day, more water and less orange juice; drink water and keep flushing, guys, keep flushing," she pleaded.

She mostly wanted us to have dinner together, but it was challenging because she wanted to have dinner at six in the evening, and that was too early for me and Vincent, her grandson. When I had classes at the university and came home late, she would prepare food for me. I would find my food on the kitchen counter or the dining table with a note on a piece of paper by its side, "Ben, here is your dinner. You can heat it if it has cooled down. The ketchup, salt, pepper, etc., are all in the cupboard above your head from the sink. And please, do not forget to clean the dining table and your plate, good night! Mom."

My host Mom is an immaculate woman and a caring mother. She is as hygienic as possible. She is no doubt the cleanest person I have ever met in my whole life. She genuinely wanted cleanliness and repeatedly ordered me to wash my hands as she did when I first moved into her house and wanted a piece of the orange chicken. She required me to wash my hands at least a million times during my two-year stay at her home. She was never shy at ordering anyone visiting or staying at her house to wash their hands regularly. She would highlight, "washing hands properly is not difficult, and it would save us from many unwanted conditions because it would protect us and others from sickness. Many sicknesses like food poisoning, cold, eye diseases, and infections would disappear."

She said, "If you can prevent some diseases by washing your hands clean; that would help you save some money, too."

The rule of washing hands applies to every person entering her house—the visitors, the guests, the travelers, etc. The multiple hand washings caused the skin of my hands to become lighter than the skin on the rest of my arms and body. She was very suitable to have me or the visitors wash our hands on every occasion. We use our hands in every activity and task and touch our noses, eyes, books, phones, door handles, pens, and car wheels. We touch so many unclean things, yet we never mind washing them properly before approaching our meal. The hand washing she recommended was not the one everybody does every day, all day. It is about hand washing, which involves applying soap repeatedly, rubbing hands together, and sometimes scrubbing for about half a minute or an entire minute.

One day, I said, "But, Mom, many people at my university, when they use the restroom, do not use all those techniques and do not wash their hands for that long."

She responded, "That is why many people are sick, and that is why they pick up a bug now and then."

"Many people do not realize it until it's too late, and others never realize it," she regretted.

"Am I allowed to take that much time in the public toilet?" I asked.

"You have to do whatever is in your power to keep healthy," she told me, "If you don't take good care of yourself, nobody will do it for you."

When food was ready, especially during dinner time, Mom called, "Ben? Vincent? Food is ready, and wash your hands, please!"

In the mornings, we did not have breakfast together. Vincent left for his construction work as early as five or six. Mom would call out at the top of her voice so I could hear her from my bedroom on the first floor, "Ben, your breakfast is on the table, and please don't forget to wash your hands." When she came from Costco, she would bring some delightful treats but only give them to you once you washed your hands after unloading the car. She would put a slice of pizza or a burrito on the counter, "You need to wash your hands before touching it." Even after I walked downstairs randomly to get something from the kitchen, she would ask, "Have you washed your hands? Please wash your hands in the kitchen sink before getting drinks or food." When I returned from school, and she was still awake, she would say, "Ben, how was class today? Wash your hands, please."

It was an important lesson that I learned. It became a precious life lesson for me, my family, friends, students, etc. It even became invaluable when the COVID-19 pandemic hit the whole world. Any time I started reading the COVID-19 guidelines, I recall my stay at her house. While the guidelines were a new way of life for others, they were a "déjà vu" for me and people with whom I have already shared my experience.

Fridays were laundry days, and Mom urged us to bring our dirty clothes downstairs and put them in front of the laundry room on Thursday afternoons.

Initially, she asked Thursday morning, "What day is tomorrow?"

"Friday," I would answer.

"What is up on Friday?" would be her question.

"Laundry," I would reply quickly.

"Don't forget to bring your clothes down, especially your bed sheets," she said.

She would get mad at around eight in the evening of Thursdays when Vincent or I or one of us forgot to bring clothes downstairs.

"You need to be organized, and I can't keep telling you all the time to bring them down."

Saturdays were cleanup days in the house, with the bathroom being the number one priority. Mom required that our bathroom be as clean as our bedrooms.

"Use the detergent and wash the tub and the wall of the tub," "Rub and scrub using your elbow power." she would insist.

I always went into the bathroom to clean the mirror, toilet, top, and ball all around the inside and outside, scrub the tub, and mope the floor.

Mom bought some electric room freshener dispensers and gave me one for use in my room. She constantly reminded me to use the air freshener, "It will keep the air in your room fresh and clean." She also wanted me to open my bedroom windows regularly to get natural light in and keep air flowing when studying or leaving for the supermarket.

"I cannot accept that your room stinks; keep it lighted and maintain airflow daily," she required.

And you need to smell good all the time, use deodorant and perfume to chase away those body odors, especially after you sweat, "you do not want people around you to avoid you, look at you weird, or pinch their nose when they get close to you, be pleasant," she pleaded.

"Gargle with water, peroxide, and salt," Mom recommended once when I came down from a light cold and coughing.

"I do not know what that means," I said.

"It means to wash one's mouth and throat with liquid that is kept in motion by breathing through it with a gurgling sound," she responded.

I still did not quite understand and stood there looking at her wondering.

She said, "Take some lukewarm water in a cup, put some peroxide and salt in it, and take a mouthful of it and gargle and spit it out."

She said gargling with salt water will allow the saline solution to coat one's mouth and throat. She added that it helps loosen mucus, lessen inflammation, and ease throat pain.

"It will also improve oral health and hygiene," She insisted, "get those food particles out before they get rotten in your throat.

It did help me every time I did. I was much relieved whenever I gargled.

I have noticed that the Portland weather is generally mild (milder). I come from a country where the climate is usually hot for most of the year, and the temperature rises as much as forty-five degrees in the dry season sometimes and falters between twenty-two and twenty-eight degrees in the rainy season. It can get as low as eighteen degrees in the cold season between mid-October and February. As of mid-August, the time of my arrival in Portland was terrific. One of the beautiful things about Portland is that it genuinely represents all four seasons. In the fall, you see gorgeous tall trees mixed with leaves that shine bright yellow and deep browns of every shade. It starts to chill two weeks in during October until mid-November.

Winter feeling comes around November. There are some rains, but the sky is cold and clear. In the fall, upon my arrival, there were picnics and barbecues in almost every green space that I could notice while driving around with my host Mom or walking around on foot and while working out. Initially, she would move me around to help me settle in. She was happy to drive me around so I could get familiar with the city and the transportation system. She first took me to a barbecue at her daughter's house in downtown Portland, where I had spent the first few nights of my stay. It was a pleasant late afternoon, and when we arrived, there were already a handful of guests. The guests were happy to see me. A big woman stood by the barbecue grill, and the other guests stood by the tables covered with blue plastic tablecloths. They had plates and Styrofoam cups in their hands. There was no doubt that Everybody liked enjoying the meat. They would get some pieces, eat them while walking around, or sit down around the table with others and enjoy it. There was also a table with soft drinks. Some of the homemade drinks were too sweet for me.

I was not used to seeing people eating meat for hours on end. I grew up eating meat after having dinner or lunch, mainly two or three pieces. I only see people eating a lot of meat during feasts like Christmas, Easter, Tabaski, Ramadan, etc. On some occasions wedding ceremonies. Seeing people eat meat in bulk on a regular day like this was quite a shock. A lot of red meat exposed in a family yard was never heard of. Overeating meat was associated with overweight, obesity, heart disease, diabetes, joint discomfort, etc. I liked the meat but consumed a moderate quantity to allow easy digestion and care for my stomach and bowels.

My honeymoon in Portland was over a couple of weeks after my arrival. I have been to picnics and barbecues and even visited the Canon beach. I enjoyed the best ice cream in the world on my way there. I had to focus on my studies. I met my academic advisor, Dr. Samuel, and registered for classes he had suggested and recommended. I had already bought some of the textbooks mentioned in the syllabus. I had even started to read some of them. As an international student whose first, second, and third language is not English, it is better to have a head start. On my first day of class, I arrived twenty minutes earlier. There were already a few undergraduate students in the classroom. I looked around the school and saw a table in the corner of the room where two American students were seated.

I approached them, greeted them with a low voice, and sat down. I was anxious. The American students exchanged a few looks with me and continued their conversation as if nobody was sitting beside them. A few moments later, the professor, Dr. Samuel, my academic advisor, walked into the classroom. He is very tall, probably six feet six, and well-bred. He was carrying a video camera. He took some time to introduce himself and asked us to do the same. He used his video camera to shoot each of us separately while we introduced ourselves to the rest of the class.

When he finished the shooting, he assured us, "The videos will stay with me, and none of us or anyone else in this world will be able to see these videos again."

Some of us giggled at his words, while others laughed out loud. I was very uncomfortable with the video recording because I was camera shy, but I managed to do it. My first classes were challenging, with many readings, assignments, tests, and presentations. The task was difficult. I had to take painkillers to relieve the headache I had been experiencing for the first few weeks. But as time went by, it became less challenging with the readings, the class presentations, and the projects, which were more comfortable for the rest of my graduate studies.

Classes at the university in the United States were different. They are more hands-on and interactive. Unlike my usual experience, we sat, crossed our legs and arms, and listened to the teachers only. We were not considered to be a clean slate in the US. We were not like empty vases into which teachers poured in. You do not have to clap your hands or fingers to have the professor's attention; you can raise your hands. Class attendance and participation have some percentage to complete the final grade. There are lots of reading materials, which, at the beginning, caused me to be restless.

I asked my academic advisor, "Do I need to read every chapter in all the books?"

He convincingly responded, "Yes, Benjamin, for each class, two to three chapters."

"Do the same next week and the following week. Follow the directives in the syllabus until the end of the quarter," He added.

I told him, "I am taking some painkillers already because of too much reading."

"There is no slowing down. Keep going; you will be fine after some time," The academic advisor, Dr. Samuel, assured.

I accompanied my host Mom to the tree farm to buy a fresh Christmas tree for my first-ever Christmas in the United States. As we were driving down to the farm, I could see the leaves of the trees by the roadside carrying some snowflakes. The snowflakes dropped as a light wind blew in the early morning hours.

We were welcomed by the owner, who was very joyful and talkative. That is all I could remember from him. I was so focused on looking at the trees and interested in learning about them that I could not have had so much time to exchange with the owner and know him more. There was a gallery of big, medium, and miniature Christmas trees. My host Mom allowed me to pick one for my first Christmas at her house. I looked around for some time while pacing up and down. I saw one beautiful medium-sized tree. I knew that I had to impress my host Mom and the guests coming over at Christmas with my choice.

I said, "Hey, Mom, this one."

She came over and was pleased and impressed with my choice. She said, "I would have chosen the same tree."

We picked up the tree, paid the owner, wrapped it up, and put it in the car trunk. We drove home, put the tree in a vase, and placed it in the hall.

The family enjoys Christmas. So, we took time to vacuum clean the rug and dust clean the wall-mounted shelves and the platforms in the living room. As we were cleaning the wall-mounted rack, I started to move objects from it one after another. I went towards the fireplace to remove and dust clean the shelf there.

That was when my host Mom came running at me and yelling, "Do not touch the urn! Do not touch the urn!"

I asked, "Why cannot I touch it? What is the problem with the urn, Mom?" She responded, "There is a souvenir in there".

My host Mom had an urn sitting on the wall mounted self in the living room with the ashes of her late son in it. Her son passed away a few years back, and she had kept an urn containing his ashes. I come from Mali, in Africa, and this practice is nonexistent there. But some people in America keep the ashes of their loved ones in their houses.

I said, "Mom, you should have told me about this. When I moved in from your daughter's, we HAD AN ORIENTATION, but you never mentioned the urn, Mom."

She responded, "You are right, but now you know about it."

That left me panting momentarily in the living room by the sofas and the armchairs.

I enjoyed the food, welcomed the guests, and exchanged smiles while sitting around the dining table in front of the kitchen. I happily accepted the gifts from my host Mom and her guests, but I always had an eye on the urn sitting on the self. For the rest of my stay in her house, I only entered the second living room on special occasions like Christmas, Easter, Thanksgiving, and birthday parties.

I was having breakfast with my host Mom. We were having some conversation as usual. We always had discussions about how often we had breakfast together. I liked the neighborhood and enjoyed the house. I knew that owning or buying a home was expensive.

I asked her, "How long has she lived in the house?"

She replied, "I have lived here for over a decade."

"How much did you pay for it?" I asked, "Was it costly?"

She thought momentarily, "It is costly. I am still paying it every month."

Out of curiosity, I asked, "Where did you get the money? How did you manage to save so much money? What did you do as a job?"

"I worked at different places doing different things," her smile faded. "I paid most of the cost of this house by selling my body part," she let it out.

"Body parts, which body parts?" I see that you have all your body parts..."

She responded, "They do not have the body parts yet."

"But they paid the money, and you used it already," I asked.

"That is correct." She responded with a severe face.

"Who bought them? What are they going to do with them?" I asked again.

"They will give my body organs to people who might need them to survive," she replied.

"So are they going to cut parts of your body to give it to the one needing it?"

"No," she replied, "they will remove the organs sold from my body after I have died.

I was freaked out. She told me that she told her children to view her dead body when she dies before her organs are taken away. She told me that she needed the money to buy her house and tomb space by her Mom and dad's tomb. I knew buying a house was expensive, but I never imagined one had to buy their tomb space. She said that she wanted to be laid by the side of her Dad and Mom's tomb. So she had to buy the area. Isn't that something?

I did not expect to befriend an old American man when traveling there. I mean an older man of eighty-plus years. The second Sunday after my arrival, my host Mom took me to her church and introduced me to some senior members, men, and women, of the church just before the beginning of the Sunday service. Among them was that white-haired older man whose name was Kernan Bagley. After the service, this man who did not know me from Adam approached me and asked many questions. He was so much interested in learning more.

He asked, "Where are you from originally?" "What country are you from, I mean?"

"I am from Mali, a country in West Africa," I responded.

"So, you are from Africa..."

"Yes, from Mali, Africa is the Continent." "Many people generalize things; Africa has about fifty-three countries, and one of them is Mali, where I come from."

"And where are you going to school?" he asked.

"I am going to PSU," I said.

"That's good," he said. He was surprisingly impressed by how I managed to travel to the United States of America for my study endeavors. He took some time to talk about himself and his family a little. He is tall, very light-skinned, and a healthy man. Over time, I discovered he is a hardworking, highly skilled, and meticulously organized older man. He is a workaholic. The work he did kept him in excellent shape physically in his eighties. Even after the doctor had told him to go home and rest, he always worked. Undoubtedly, his work ethic made him the successful man he is today. He traveled to many states throughout the United States. He was a prisoner's escort and met President Ronald Reagan during his prime years for excelling in prisoner escorting. I heard from the community that he was, in fact, the first black man in the state of Oregon to meet the President of the United States at the white house.

He deserved it through his dedication and hard work. He fondly talked about it a few weeks after we met while driving to the church together to mow the lawn. He also worked as a car dealer and is savvy in car brands, car sales, car maintenance, car transporting, etc. He just loved cars. He has a Corvette comfortable sitting in his garage and always says it is one of the fastest cars in the world. He regularly told me it goes as fast as two hundred miles per hour.

He first wanted me to help him with his weekly lawn mowing activities. We occasionally mowed the lawn together at his house and his son's on-lease house. We also did the lawn at the church every week, either Friday afternoon or Saturday morning. The church had a push lawn mower and a riding one.

During these mowing activities, he came up to me and asked me, "Who taught you how to work like you do?"

I responded with a question, "What do you mean?"

With a smile, he said, "Your work is clean, neat, and thorough."

"I was born and raised to work hard and neatly," I said.

"I see why," he said.

He was impressed with my way of working since the first day we started. I did not know that he tried to do these lawn-mowing activities with a few gentlemen he knew, but it has yet to work out. The young people he tried to do the work with only showed up sometimes when they were needed. They either botched the work or did untidy jobs when they showed up. Sometimes, they stopped working in the middle of an activity to go away or found excuses not to be available when work was there for them. He concluded that most young people were as lazy as sloths. Most did not like to work but wanted to have money and be rich one day. They generally wanted easy money. So, he decided to leave them alone and carried out the job alone for quite some time until I arrived in the community.

On Sunday, when people came to church, they would greatly appreciate the work done on the lawn. My friend would then say, "Thank this young man; he always does a great job. God bless you, my son! I don't know how you did it, and I don't care. You are a good person no matter what other people say," he would joke this way while talking with the other elders of the church.

He is a millionaire nowadays, a self-made millionaire, and started very low in terms of work and pay. He did not go to school for long. He dropped out somewhere after he graduated from high school. He was hired as a cleaner in an office building and was tasked with cleaning the boss's office. He was clean and neat in his everyday cleaning job.

When he entered the boss's office, he said, "I looked with concentration at the items on his desk. I removed the items, cleaned the desk, and put them back in their specific place," He recalled. And when the boss came the next day, everything in the office was clean, and everything was in its usual place. It happened repeatedly over time. The boss called him into his office one day and asked if he went to school. He responded that he was studying for an associate degree but dropped out. His boss told him that he was doing so well at his job. His boss upgraded him. Over the years, he worked continuously hard and efficiently to obtain the position of prisoner's escort, which allowed him to meet the President of the United States, Ronald Reagan, a resident of the white office in the eighties.

Mister Bagley and I enjoyed working together for the rest of my stay. We sometimes had breakfast with his sons at his second and younger son's houses, about forty-five miles from downtown Portland. Every time we planned to go there for breakfast, he would tell me ahead of time to be ready by six o'clock. When he arrived at my host Mom's house, I would come out so we could drive away. On our first breakfast day, I was ready, waiting for him and looking out of my window, which gave me a view of the street. I would be able to see him arriving from my room. At the sight of his car turning the corner, I ran downstairs to meet him at the entrance. He was like I told you to be ready at six o'clock.

I said, "As you can see, I am ready."

He said, "No, you aren't." He playfully complained, "You are ready means standing at the door by the roadside waiting to get in the car as soon as I pulled up in front of you."

He said, "I should not be parking my car and waiting for you at the entrance while you walked down the stairs. Ready means you are ready to jump in the car when I pull up."

I said, "Well noted, sir, you are completely right." I added, "I am not used to doing that, but I am happy I have learned something new today."

He gleefully said, "Good for you."

I had to add a new dimension to my life. After that short life lesson, we drove to his son's house for our first breakfast.

We drove there now and then during my stay. It was fun and exciting driving down there. Every time we went down, and I was at the wheel, he would order me to put the car on cruise control as soon as we got on the highway. So, I would do as he said when I reached my desired speed within the legal limit. When I did that, he would tell me to sit back and relax. He insisted that I put the vehicle on cruise control whenever I was on the highway because it would reduce fuel consumption and make the car very stable.

I was already a Mali driver's license holder when I traveled to the United States. However, I had to retake the test to be able to drive in the US. When my host Mom told Bagley, during the after-Sunday service talk, that I was planning to take the test, he was open to help as much as he could with my renewed challenge. He would pick me up so we could practice driving around the city in his pickup truck. He would choose complicated driving areas and put me to practice for some time in these areas. He made me do things like parking in tight spaces, driving in front of supermarkets where the stop signs are painted on the floor, etc.

When I drove past the street in front of the mall, he would say, "What is the problem with you? Don't you see the stop sign just in front of you?"

"I am not paying attention to the floor," I said. "I was looking on the sides focused on the road signs."

He softly said, "Road signs can also be on the floor. You need to pay attention to the floor the same way you pay attention to the signs on the roadside."

"Thanks a lot for opening my eyes to that," I said.

Sometimes, he would throw himself on me purposely when I turned a corner abruptly.

He would say, "Turn slowly and smoothly, young man; one day, you will be driving your wife, and you would not want her to fall all over you as I did. You need to be a gentle and kind man."

On some occasions, he would check to see if I was speeding up or not.

He would recommend, "Please adopt good driving habits now. If you do not create the habits in yourself that will make you stable now, you will always have issues in traffic."

He warned me not to keep my hand at a twelve o'clock position when taking the driving test. I needed to have both hands well positioned on the steering wheel; if not I would fail even before starting it.

While driving, he asked, "Do you see the traffic light ahead?" I would respond that, "Yes, I do. It is green."

He said, "But it has been green for some time, which means it will probably turn orange and red by the time you get there."

I said, "Alright."

He said. "So, slow down before you are in trouble."

Sometimes, when there was a lot of traffic, he would say, "Always look at the second or third, fourth car ahead of you in line. When you see their stop light, you should get ready to step on the brake as well."

He begged, "Do not look and wait for only the car right before you to hit the brake and go for it."

Two weeks before I passed my test to receive my US driver's license, he took me out to an empty space. We drove there together in the morning time. When we got there, he gave me the steering wheel. He was about to put me to something I had never had the opportunity to do. He told me to drive to the other part of the wall. He ordered me to turn round and face where I came from. I turned around and saw a vast piece of land before me. He told me to bring the car to a very high speed. His car was a Toyota Pick Up and was in excellent shape. I brought the car to a very high speed.

When the car was at almost the peak of speed, he promptly asked, "Slam on the brake!"

I asked, "What? What did you say?"

He ordered again, "Step on brake as hard as you can, son."

I did, and the car came to a screeching halt. I asked him why he was doing such a thing, and he said he was testing to see if I was bold enough to do something like that.

He said, "Imagine you are in traffic, and a car abruptly stops before you. You need to step so hard on the brake to bring the car to a sudden stop. If not, you will have a nasty and even deadly accident."

He told me never to strike on the brake for fear of anything.

He insisted, "It is there to be stepped on, so step on to save lives."

He told me about the severe accident his daughter was involved in because she refused to step hard on the brake to bring the car to a sudden stop.

After the braking sessions, he made me do parallel parking sessions. He said I needed only three moves for you to park the car in a parallel position between two cars. Since no cars were around in parallel positions, he placed stones to represent the two cars. I repeated the process until I could easily park in just three moves.

For the rest of the practice sessions, over the rest of the week, he put the final touches to his coaching task. He told me things such as acting right every time. He wanted me to believe I was the only good driver on the road.

He insisted, "If you consider yourself the only good driver; that will save you from many unwanted situations."

"I copied it," I responded.

He added, "Be ready to yield to the ambulance, wheelchairs, and pedestrians."

He insisted that I must also be patient with slow drivers, like senior people at the wheel, and avoid road rages. Regarding pedestrians, he was very strict and firm in his coaching. "Leave enough room before overtaking them; you will put them in hospitals for the rest of their life if you do not respect that rule," he would say with a grave face.

"Do not ever play with the rules when it comes to pedestrians. You may rot in prison for breaking them," He said, "so please abide by that rule."

"Yes, sir!" I said.

"And please look for cyclists who might come in the back on your right before turning," he insisted.

I retorted, "Aren't they supposed to stop and let us turn?"

He replied vehemently, "No, they aren't."

"When you hear an ambulance, please stop where you are until the ambulance overtakes you and goes its way," he recommended.

Ambulances are always prioritized: "You do not know which direction they are going, so you stop where you are and let them go their way."

If not, you can cause accidents. You can only make things worse if you keep driving or try to help them out. They do not need your help. They only need the road ahead of them or the exit roads, so stay put where you are.

As he is used to saying, "You are the only sane driver in the entire traffic," he persuaded me to think this way.

He recommended that I never forget, "Everybody else is a bad driver, everybody else is a lousy driver, and everybody else is a crazy driver except yourself. You are the only driver with one hundred percent control of your car, and you have all the reflexes in your environment. Never count on other drivers to save you, be quite vigilant, or have perfect control of their cars."

"Never expect other drivers to be alert at all times; you do not know what they are going through, so please do not expect them to be just fine. Just be cool with yourself," he convinced me.

Whenever we drove home from work or his son's house after breakfast, he would ask the same questions repeatedly every time we turned to enter our street.

"Do you see the white dotted lines," he would ask.

I would ask, "Which dotted lines are you talking about?" He would say, "The ones in the middle of the roads before you."

I would answer that "there were no lines."

He said, "Every good driver sees those imaginary dotted lines."

"You should not drive and overstep on them, even though the lines are invisible. One should know the limit as a driver because it is a two-way road," He said.

When I first arrived in the United States, I was approached by people asking me to give them odd amounts of dollars, payments such as five cents, ten cents, one dollar, and twenty-five cents. And these people were either at the bus stop or train stations. I also noticed people under the bridges with sheets around their waists, some living in tents and others in their cars. I was shocked to learn that most of them were homeless people. I could not fathom that homeless people are still in the most powerful and prosperous countries like the United States. As poor as people are in my country, they do not lack the basic needs of living quarters. I could not imagine how these people spent nights in the cold, rain, and wind. I could not just figure out why these poor people were out there while others had an abundance of riches.

Many rich people around this country see the plight of these homeless people, but they stay quiet and unmoved. The picture I had of this country before coming and the one I had after my arrival were two very different pictures. I could not see the image of hospitality and solidarity I used to see back in my culture. It was inconceivable to me. Were all these people outside by choice? Were they there for lack of means? Or were they there due to destiny?

My host Mom had her grandson pay rent and money for food to allow him to stay in her house. That was the first ever cultural shock I experienced. It proves the point why a lot of people end up in the streets. The day her grandson cannot pay for rent and food, he will belong to the streets. It is quite a big shock for someone from a country where solidarity and hospitality are common daily. Grandmas must do more than charge grandsons for providing living quarter services or any services. This practice is believed to be greedy and unacceptable in my culture. People live in extended families; therefore, there is enough space to house everyone, and enough food is provided to feed all family members.

Thanksgiving is an occasion for millions of American families to celebrate the past year's good harvest and other blessings.

I rode the bus to the barbershop downtown Portland in the morning for a haircut. I returned home around ten in the morning to help prepare for Thanksgiving Day. I also kept in mind the next day, which was Black Friday. My host family had relatives and friends come over for Thanksgiving Dinner. It was my first time to be part of an event typically American. So, just before the dinner, we were all gathered in the living room. My host Mom asked people to say something about themselves, their family, friends, etc. Some say they are thankful for their family life and finding a new job; others are thankful for overcoming their health issues and many other things.

After all the guests had spoken, she asked me, "What about you, young man?"

Naturally, I said, "I decided not to speak."

Well, for me, it is all right to say such a thing, but immediately following my statement, the living room was full of some astonishments, and some of them were dismayed and looking at me strangely.

And then my host Mom said, "Hey, young man, "this is what we do in America."

She and the guests considered me "I decided not to speak" an act of ungratefulness to God, which was very wrong on their behalf. The most shocking thing was not the fact that they did not know that Thanksgiving Day does not exist in my culture, but it was the fact that nobody got the idea to ask me the question to find out why I decided to say anything openly.

I am grateful to God every single day. Some people in the living room seemed like they did not care about other people's culture, and I could not believe it. It was embarrassing and disappointing for me. In addition, I was reading a book titled "Lies My Teacher Told Me" by Loewen, which describes how history textbooks distort the facts about Thanksgiving. This information made me cautious about Thanksgiving as well.

The following day, Black Friday, I went to Fred Meyer with them (the host family) to shop. The night before, they had already told me that on Black Friday, items were off in many places and that if I wanted, I could go with them to do some shopping. I agreed and was eager to go with them the following day. I liked and enjoyed shopping while I was in my country. I noted down what I needed to buy before going there. What I did not know, however, is that shopping in America is not what I thought it would be, especially shopping on a Black Friday.

Once at Fred Meyer, everybody went their way after agreeing to meet at the counter within a couple of hours. So, when we met at the counter to check out, Mom realized I had a few items in my shopping cart. She looked perplexed, gazing at me.

She asked, "What is this?"

I said, "What?"

She said, "Is that all you bought?"

And I said, "Yes, that is all I needed."

The next thing she did was to turn to a lady standing next to her to gesture for her to see what I had in my shopping cart.

She turned back to me and said bluntly and with a commanding voice, "This is America, and Americans buy a lot on Black Friday to save money," she added, "When in Rome, do as Romans do."

She meant I needed to do the American way regardless of my needs. I asked myself, do I have to buy things I did not need just because it is Black Friday or because many items are at a discount? That cannot be right; it is not fair at all. It embarrassed me, and I was very frustrated, but I did not blame them because it was the right thing to do for them.

My host Mom took me to senior people's houses a few times so I could see how these people lived. She taught me to be ready psychologically when we get there.

She warned, "You know when people get older, they do not necessarily smell good, put up with them and approach them and offer your support by hugging them and shaking hands with them."

"I can cope with that," I assured her.

Mom said, "After they eat food, their body releases some unpleasant odor through their mouth. They don't have perfect hygiene, you know."

"But one day, you told me people were available to care for them. Why aren't these people doing their job?" I asked.

She looked at me and said, "They cannot provide all that care; they are doing business and need the money."

After silence, Mom sadly said, "It is not a job genuinely done."

It did shock me to see senior people in these conditions while their grown-up children were living in the city. It is a monotonous and boring life. It looked like a routine every single day. It made me very sad to see older people live in retirement homes while they have grown up and have successful children who can care for them by keeping them in their space.

In my society, older people are cared for by their grown-up children. It is considered a real curse when grown-up children fail to live with and care for their parents.

My father told me how the senior people's housing thing came to be. He heard it from the American missionaries when he was a service boy and later a pastor student. He learned from them that a confident man took his old and dying father away from his home and laid him under a tree. The reason was because he had lived his life, and it was time for him to die. He left him under a tree by the roadside with little food and water like an animal. His father would use the food and water and die after or before he could even use either the food or the water.

The same man, when he became old and very sick, his son took him away and left him under a tree just like he had left his father a while back. While his son was going, he called and told him not to do so. He told his son that he had done the same thing to his Dad, who was his grandfather. He begged his son to take him back with him and find another solution. If not, the same thing would happen to him when he got old, and the cycle would continue forever.

That is when his son changed his mind, took him back with him, and put him in a house where he provided him with the necessities until he died. Soon, the practice was stopped. That is when assisted-living communities came to be.

I was relieved when my host Mom told me she had no pets. We did not have a pet in our house back home either. Dad never liked pets, especially dogs, because he had only one blood sister, who died from a wound from a dog bite. So, whenever he saw a dog, it reminded him of his sister's pain. I visited many American families with dog pets; some loved their dogs more than anything, sometimes more than their parents. I could not imagine myself loving pets more than my people.

My host Mom warned, "Please tell pet owners that you like their pets. Say their pets are nice and all."

"You can count on me on that," I promised.

Mom said, "If you openly show them you do not like their pet, they will hate you."

I shook my head, "I know how these games are played."

My host Mom told me she knew a lady who wrote her will on behalf of her pet dog and willed all her assets to her dog after she passed away.

My host Mom invited me and her grandson Vincent to the buffet in downtown Portland a few times. The first time, we went there to celebrate Vincent's birthday. She paid thirty dollars something for the three of us. We went there late in the afternoon for about an hour. It was very busy when we arrived. They welcomed us and made us seated. We waited a moment and got clearance to serve ourselves. There were all kinds of food, some of which I liked were fried plantain, chicken, guinea fowl, etc. Others, like frogs, snails, oysters, etc., were the ones I disliked. We did not eat those foods in my culture. I told myself I would not return to my country upon graduation and told my people I had been eating frogs, snails, etc. People would be laughing their heads off.

My host Mom was not very happy about me and Vincent.

She said, "You guys wasted my time, money, and effort."

She felt unhappy because we did not eat much after she had paid thirty bucks or more. From then on, Mom had us prepared beforehand if we were going to buffet.

One day, right after I arrived home from the university and headed into my room, Mom knocked at my door. I opened the door, and she said, "Do not eat now because we are going to the buffet."

I asked, "Are we going right now?"

She replied, "Sometime in the late afternoon."

So I said, "Can I at least have a little bite before the late afternoon?"

She said, "Negative."

She said, "I am not going to throw my money by taking you there if you are not profiting from the occasion."

A few minutes later, she called me downstairs. She said she wanted to teach me something about eating. She said there are occasions when one should eat at a very slow pace. For instance, when we go to a buffet to pay an amount of money for several people, we should take our time. Taking time to eat makes one enjoy their food more, and it is healthier because one takes time to chew on it.

When one eats slowly, food tastes better, and one can eat more, "Do not waste my money this time around," she concluded as the final verdict.

Many teenagers and adolescents wearing strange clothes, carrying tattoos, and having body piercings were seen pacing up and down at bus stops, train stations, and local parks. There was no modesty at all in the way they appeared. Why expose your private body to anybody out there when you are supposed to have a husband or a wife to whom you should be committed? You reveal your body to be looked at but sue people for harassment when they look at you. These things are considered to be impractical in my culture. Only women are supposed to pierce their bodies, but even that, it is not any body part. They are expected to wear earrings, and some women also pierce their lower lips, but that is all.

I was also surprised that my host family needed help understanding my attitude regarding some American foods. Food like gumbo is unknown in my culture; I have never had it before. I had not even heard about gumbo in the past, but my host family was very surprised and disappointed at Thanksgiving when I kindly refused to eat. For me, it is normal for someone to resist eating foods that are unfamiliar to them. Still, unfortunately, my host family failed to understand my resistance vis-à-vis some American foods.

In addition, it is shocking to me to see how people in America are so attached to sweet foods. Almost every meal is accompanied by sweets such as cookies, chocolates, cakes, and the like, and that is why many people are overweight, probably, and many others are obese. Many have no control over what goes into their mouth. My host Mom believed that since I came from a developing world and living conditions in my country were far less attractive than what they had, they wanted me to accept their food and drinks without question.

I accompanied my host Mom to many social events. I have attended church regularly. I noticed a lot of single moms with children at these events with no fathers or men around. It is less common in my culture. I wondered why all these women had all the children that they had, but they did not have a husband. Are they all widows? Are their husbands military men on overseas duty? Are these women's husbands so busy working that they do not have time to spend with their wives and children? It is uncommon to see a single family headed by a woman. Well, a woman alone is not expected to be able to give a decent education to children or be able to build the character, resilience, discipline, and self-confidence that a child needs to develop and overcome challenges in life—children who are supposed to become Alpha males and lead their own families in the future. Women are expected to have a family life while being married to a man who is the family's stronghold. A man's voice is needed in the household.

But I was very impressed by how many people showed their love by offering hugs. Whenever I attended church service with my friend or host Mom, many hugged me to show they were pleased to meet me. It is not common in my culture to embrace people; people usually offer hugs when a very sad or happy event occurs to show their feelings, but even in those cases, only a few people do it. People did show their love every time but through their everyday actions, behavior, and attitude. Sometimes, it is inappropriate to offer hugs. It is undoubtedly a way of proving the love people may have for each other.

I have seen many American people smile and talk easily to strangers, sharing personal stories while I was riding the buses or trains to and from school. Special seats in the front of buses are reserved for disabled people or senior citizens—something I admire and appreciate because it is true in my culture, too.

One day, I was riding the yellow line in the evening. There were not many people inside, and I was sitting on the seat by the train door, searching my phone. At the next train stop, an older man entered and stood next to me. It looked like he had difficulty walking properly. I offered him my seat even though there were empty seats behind me. I walked back a few rows and sat on one of the seats. A woman was riding with us. She was standing by her bike hanging from the bike hangers. She looked exhausted and seemed to have a long and hectic day. She approached me and said, "Thank you so very much for offering your seat to him." She offered me a significant smile. She did not know me or the older man from Adam, but she was glad that I showed him my seat.

I visited the family of a man, a member of the church I attended. It was a visit. We dropped by his house when he came around to pick me up at my host's house so we could buy some items from the supermarket for the next potluck at our church. He lived in downtown Portland, and his house was located in a clean, peaceful, and quiet neighborhood. When I accompanied him inside the house, it seemed empty to me. I was expecting to meet his children, but they were not there. Out of curiosity, I almost asked where the kids were, but I had self-controlled it and kept it for myself. I realized that only his overweight wife was inside the house. As soon as we entered, she came out of the bedroom, exchanged greetings with me, and sat on the first sofa closest to her. We already knew each other because she regularly attended church like me.

Her husband said since we had all day to do the shopping, he would like to cook some food for lunch before we could go to make the purchases. I agreed, and he took a pie plate, a knife, a spoon, some brown sugar, some granulated sugar, some lemon juice, some cinnamon, some nutmeg, some flour, etc. from the cupboard. He went to the kitchen counter to get some apples he brought to the dining table. He sliced the apples and gently tossed the apple slices, the granulated sugar, the brown sugar, the cinnamon, the nutmeg, the lemon zest, and the juice until it was well combined and set aside. Then he preheated the oven to four hundred Fahrenheit. He took the pie crust discs from the fridge and kept them on the dining table for a few minutes. He then rolled one disc, placed it into a deep dish pie plate, and evenly spread the apple slices. Next, he moved the second disc and covered the apple pie filling. He trimmed the excess of dough. He then placed the pie dish onto the baking sheet. He baked it for about twenty to twenty-five minutes and then another twenty minutes after removing the shield. All this happened when his wife sat on the sofa using her phone. I noticed that many American men do their best to share equally with their wives in parenting and housework.

I am from a culture where husbands do not equally share with their wives in parenting and doing the housework. Certain types of work are done mostly by women, and women only expect men to do those works if there are critical situations like sickness and prolonged absences. Tasks such as cooking, cleaning the house, doing the laundry, and caring for the babies are even believed to be innate skills inherent only to women. Most of the time, men are considered the breadwinners and the dominant figure, the leader, provider, and protectors of the household. If a man is caught doing such a thing that is labeled female, he is believed to be very weak and sometimes even a coward. They will, therefore, lose the esteem of their fellow men and other members of the society.

My spell in America revealed that culture is complex and challenging to understand. As a human being, one can only accept and embrace things appropriate to one's culture. Therefore, anything that complies with one's culture is correct. I learned that as an educator, I am called to be careful, be on the lookout, be tactful, and not be harmful to anyone in my speech, behavior, gesture, or anything else. Being an educator is a very complex band daunting profession. As a teacher, one meets various people and learners from all over the world, and all of them are as different as the places and locations they all come from. I learned that many people I met have different cultures than mine, and my acquisitions shaped my personality and contributed a lot to my ability to be a culturally responsive educator.

Portland is a bustling city, and Portland State University was full of life and welcomed thousands of students worldwide. It is the most diverse university in Oregon, and I found out during my stay there. The top countries represented at Portland State University are Saudi Arabia, China, India, Kuwait, and Japan. I came from Mali, Africa, and others came from different African countries. Diversity was noticeable throughout the campus and the entire city. Many different cultures were presented, and there was so much out there for learning on campus in general, in the classrooms, and in the entire city of Portland.

Jan Abramovitz, the professor who had the most significant impact on me during my two years of graduate studies, is a seasoned professor and is culturally both aware and very flexible. He loved teaching and fully mastered what he taught. He taught with an absolute ease. He is a physically fit, lean, and well-balanced man. He mostly wore jeans and shirts during classes, which made him younger and made him feel very comfortable. He pulled his rolling cart into the classroom and had everything he needed, especially items used in arts teaching. He is always modest in his personality. I took two classes with him--Theories of Instruction and Theoretical Models of Curriculum. He is an excellent mind reader and can tell if a student understands his teachings just by looking at the facial expressions. He is the most culturally responsive professor I have had classes with. He is always available and happy to meet his students' needs.

From the first day, I came into the class, I noticed his primary goal was to be as much as possible a culturally responsive educator. He asked students if he pronounced their names correctly and such. He thrived on helping all students become respectful of the diversity of cultures in their school environment and assisted learners in interacting better with people outside the school environment as soon as they left school. In his class, he made sure that all students were comfortable interacting with each other. The implicit factor of his being culturally responsive guided his students that differences in ways of thinking and culture are to be cherished and appreciated rather than judged and neglected. His everyday attitude showed that the best way to fight against the natural aversion to unknown beliefs and values is to provide students with enough evidence that people who do not look like them are, in spirit, just like them. He gave opportunities to students to share stories of their home lives. He asked them to share and provide information about their family holiday practices, cultural traditions, domestic holidays, cultural events, customs, etc. His interest and skills in arts help his students in many ways. I had the privilege to interview him on my master's thesis on how teaching impacted students at the university. I was very impressed with his office spaces covered with artwork. I found him in his office with the door wide open. He was preparing some art items that he could use in his next class. I waited a few minutes for him to finish preparing but soon realized he was ready to be interviewed while working. It spoke volumes.

He loved doing collages and showed his students drawings and images of people from different ethnicities, shapes, sizes, and clothing, and this provided students with the opportunity to discover people who looked different from them, their families, and their friends.

In my first semester, in the Fall of 2015, I was in his class and learned so much about how he used the book Approaches to Teaching authored by Gary D Fenstermacher and Jonas F. Soltis in his Theories to Teaching class. The three approaches in this book are the Executive, the Facilitator, and the Liberationist. These approaches equipped us, students, with the tools to shape the future of our learners. In this class, he asked the students to find an article of their choice on teaching and present it. He ensured the student could deliver according to the format he/she wanted. On the day of the presentation, he sat aside to give control of the class to the one doing their presentation. When my turn arrived, I was shaking, not from cold but from fear and anxiousness. It was the first-ever presentation for my graduate class. During the presentation, it was clear I was uncomfortable. I struggled to make eye contact with my classmates for five seconds. I even noticed the professor raising his hand for a few seconds during my presentation. He wanted to say something, but I could not give him the floor for whatever reason. Even today, I am angry for not providing him with the floor.

He firmly believed that a culturally-centered instructional approach could help facilitate cultural pride among diverse students. He took measures to adopt a neutral position as a teacher, avoided biased attitudes toward cultural issues, and made schools a better, more exciting, and more relevant place. He adopted several behavioral and instructional techniques and strategies that enabled him to build more vigorous learning and teaching relationships with culturally diverse students, and these behaviors determined and incarnated good teachings and led to academic success. He established measures to create an environment conducive to learning and an open community where learners would have freedom and safely express their disparate views despite their cultural pluralism.

He provided increased opportunities for high and low achievers to boost their self-esteem and enhance their strengths and talents. I benefitted from these rising opportunities and enhanced my motivation to learn and achieve great things. In the end, it is the question of who can emulate him. Anybody who manages to emulate his teaching and adopt his personality will become the best of the best because he has surpassed all. He liberated us by letting us know that we have the mental capability to achieve academic success. He always paid attention to other cultures' folklore, music, religion, etc.

He genuinely considered differences in students regarding their appearances, race, sex, disability, ethnicity, socioeconomic status, and ability to help create productive teaching and learning systems.

On June 18, 2017, the much-anticipated graduation was held at the Convention Center in downtown Portland. I had the right to invite five people but asked only two: my host Mom and her close friend from the church. They knew I had no relatives and would feel alone as an international student. They also came to support me at the graduation ceremony and the hooding ceremony. On the morning of the commencement, I woke and found my host Mom already waiting for me downstairs to give me some directives about how the traffic would be. She said I needed to be at the convention center as early as possible and reassured me that they would be there by the official starting time. I had breakfast with her and left.

The Convention Center was full of people. I met my classmates there, and we all walked to meet the faculty members waiting for us in the lobby. Everybody walked around and took pictures with classmates, parents, cousins, professors, etc. Most professors from the School of Education attended the commencement and hooding ceremony. I walked around aimlessly to take pictures with my classmates and professors. At the commencement, I felt it when the Portland State University president, Wim Wiewel, said: "Congratulations, Class of 2017! You did it, and we are proud of your accomplishments and hard work in earning your PSU degree. Let's take a moment to reflect on the journey. Some of you are the first in your family to attend a graduate college..." After that part, I could not concentrate anymore on the rest of his speech. I am the youngest of my family, and the only one who attended graduate school, and I did it in the leading country in the field of education, the United States of America. I felt it to the bone and the marrow. It was a significant break for me. I kept thinking about my journey at the rest of the commencement and did not notice much of the rest of the ceremony.

At the hooding ceremony in the afternoon, I had the privilege to have my academic advisor, Dr. Samuel Henry, put the hood on me. I also had the honor to stand by my employer and head of the curriculum and Instruction department, Dr. William Parnell alias Will, on the podium while I received the hood. Will took time to have a few words to thank me for working as a graduate assistant and praised me for all the excellent work, dedication, and commitment to providing services to the curriculum and education department. I felt great while he was saying these words on my behalf. He is the head of the curriculum department and my employer. It was nice of him to allow me to have work experience as an international student and to network with the faculty members at the school of education, especially in the curriculum and instruction department. I learned a whole lot of things in terms of teaching by participating and taking minutes during the GTEP, the Graduate Teachers Education Program, and faculty biweekly meeting, in terms of research by researching narrative inquiry and interview research that relates to interviewing researchers to help them hone in on their research question, and also by researching mini-grants.

I was given a memorable sending-off from my church community. After two years of dedicated service, the church organized a surprise party on my behalf to show their gratitude to me for faithfully serving them during the two years of my stay there. My host Mom told me there was a usual potluck that Sunday. So, for me, it was a potluck. When the sermon was over, I was working on the sound system and transferring and copying the sermon recording on CDs for those interested in buying them. Everybody was asked to go downstairs for the potluck. A church lady told me I was needed downstairs in the potluck room. I kept copying the sermon on the CDs and told myself I would join them when I finished the copying.

A moment later, the church's President, Mister Geither, said, "Go downstairs, Ben, go get some food."

I accepted. "there are a couple of CDs left for copying," I said while going downstairs.

He said, "I will continue doing the copying for you while you get some food; just go, Ben."

I walked down the stairs where everyone was waiting for me. I sat at a table, waiting for meal prayer before I could help myself. My host Mom was the one who was leading the potluck or the party. She walked to the other side of the room, where I could see her, and started to read the message addressed to me by the church members. I soon realized the whole thing was about me and began to cry. I went to give a hug to my best friend, Mister Bagley, who was my accomplice. They had a money tree carrying the Malian flag sitting on the table in the corner, and everybody from the church, from elders to children, put some dollar bills on the money tree.

Mister Bagley stood up, said a few words about me, and told the members how committed I was to the church and how I worked hard on behalf of the church whenever needed. He concluded that he did not care what everyone was saying and might say. He said he had a conviction that I am a good man. While driving home with the money tree behind me in the backseat, I was still under the emotions. The church members were so lovely and kind to recognize me for a small service I was giving because I love God.

CHAPTER 3

Mali Koura—New Mali

"Life never betrays if one does not show off!" is an old popular saying by African singers to warn, give advice, and teach people.

"You will never have enough," a scholar of the Griot family, known for their mastery of speech, once said. The Griots are known to be the ones who transmit the history orally from generation to generation. These people would say: "It is sweet to be offered something for free," "What is even sweeter than that is to be offered another one for free."

After I returned to my country from my study trip in the United States of America, I lived in a different neighborhood with different people than in the community I lived in before my journey. The community was animated all the time, and people seemed friendly. I lived in a building with four apartments and two single rooms for lease. All of the apartments and single rooms were leased. There was a big apartment better in appearance, which was inhabited by the family of the landlord, who himself lived in France. While the leasing apartments were of standard quality, theirs was very high, with tiled walls, oil-based paint, and plaster ceiling. Lessees enjoyed a different quality living standard than the owner's family regarding housing, furniture, and accessories.

Mambi, one of the lessees, was a blue-collar worker returning home from his work site. He and his family lived in an apartment opposite mine. I was sitting on the terrace of my apartment as usual after I returned home from the office. Since the apartments were facing each other, I could see and hear their conversation.

As soon as he got home, he said, "Phew! What a day! It was hectic!" And he sighed. He felt a gloomy atmosphere in his home. "Something is not right here," he said. He looked at Madam and asked, "Are you sick?" he followed up with another question about the children, "Are children sick, or is something wrong with them?" He could see himself that the kids were fine. He asked, "Is someone else feeling sick?" He inquired. "What is the problem?"

Madam casually responded, "There is no problem of that nature."

The husband was lost and renewed his question because his wife appeared gloomy and did not have the usual demeanor.

His wife slowly asked, "Have you forgotten my niece's wedding ceremony, which is fast approaching."

She complained that her husband was not making any arrangements for the occasion. Her husband needed to understand what arrangements his wife was talking about.

He said, "We will attend the wedding ceremony as usual. Like we always attended events on your family side, as on my family side."

She asked, "Are we going to attend the wedding just like that? No new clothes, shoes, handbags, etc."

Mambi said, "Darling, we have already talked about this, and you know my opinion and position on that."

He asked, "Why is this clothing so important to you?" He said, "Our presence is more important, the joy we will have, the solidarity we will show is far more important than those new clothes, shoes, etc."

Many people, primarily women, are obsessed with making others think they are rich and have a high status when, in reality, they are broke and barely make it by wasting the money they have on useless things to attend a wedding ceremony.

His wife said, "Are we going there like destitute people?"

But the husband quickly responded, "We are far from destitute."

He said just because they were not wearing new outfits would not mean destitute. She continued to nag him that, for her, to be honest, it was a shame to be attending a wedding ceremony with old outfits when everybody else would be wearing new outfits. The husband then did not know much to say to bring her to reality. He said things were hard, very hard indeed. He asked her to remember on all the occasions he had been buying them what they wanted over the years. His wife said she understood that, but it was different on that occasion. She finally told her husband to forget about it and that she would no longer attend the wedding. The husband murmured that he found it mind-boggling at all this nonsense and thought his wife should understand when life was treating them not well sometimes.

Daily, people are more interested in themselves than anything else. They want more, more. "The bigger you eat, the more the appetite," I fathomed. Talking in the context of my community, most people are well-dressed (bazin riche Metzger, embroidered clothes, but many of them have either been indebted or bought them with ill-gotten fortunes. Ill-gotten gains, wealth, fortunes, etc, almost lure many people into society.

Regular news is that an executive has embezzled money destined for needy people, humanitarian reasons, or a particular project. However, when you carefully consider those accused of the wrongdoings, they already have some money but want more and more. Some individuals in abject poverty are indeed involved in embezzlement, and others are far better off affected. It is greediness for most people involved in this situation, whether poor or rich. In everyday life, when I look around, I see many people in the community who look well-off in appearance.

But many people getting by life and struggling to make ends meet are seen eating in chic restaurants, riding taxis everywhere, and dressing up in lavishly purchased clothes. A lot of people suffer from this seemingly incurable syndrome. With a little increase in their income, they go with a significant increase in spending and lifestyles.

Way too many people want to live high off the hog; they eat meals at sit-down restaurants when cooking at home is cheaper. They drive their cars everywhere when public transportation will do the trick, or walking the distance is possible and contributes to better health. They buy expensive clothes when second-hand clothes from Goodwill and casual businesses will make them look good. The illusion is stark when you see where these people live. They work for two to three years and buy an iPhone with all the money they make. They will use the iPhone only for a year or two. They live in chic and attractive quarters while acting and living like this.

Even more sickening is that these people rent the nicest apartment even though they have all the difficulties in the world to pay for the rent. So, yes! These people live above their means. A saying reads: "You can afford some stuff but decide not to buy it because that is simply life." One needs to know between what is necessary and what is not. One may want something, but it is optional for the time being. Live well below your means. One needs to exercise self-control, fend off temptation, and become a minimalist.

Flabbergasting is the illusion of the younger generation, younger males and females, especially the ones between sixteen, early to mid-twenties, and even as old as late twenties. They want to live a high life, the young males in particular. It is challenging for some of us raised as males to get our life together and try not to live a high life at a young age. We were told to have a plan and get to work.

"On the one hand, money is used for luxury things such as decorations, extravagant clothes, fancy cars, and high lifestyles. On the other hand, someone does not have the means to afford a decent meal to survive." Life is unfair indeed, it seems!

In a country like mine, wedding ceremonies are events when many people show off. Wedding ceremonies are labeled "mondial" by many young people and some grown-up people. "Mondial" means global. When people say their event is "mondial", it means their event is unparalleled in terms of fame, finances, and scope; all know it and will make the front page of the Gazette the next day. Every young person wants to have a "mondial" wedding ceremony. Some save money over the years doing odd jobs and spend the whole of their saving in one day. Some others borrow money to organize their wedding ceremonies. Wedding ceremonies are events during which people try to impress others. On almost every occasion, these young people are dressed in the latest styles of clothes. In most cases, it is a uniform they wear. If there is no uniform during someone's wedding ceremony, then that wedding ceremony is not considered a "mondial" wedding. The fame of going "mondial" drives the rich and the poor to do everything they possibly or impossibly can (use every means to get money) to buy the "now" required uniforms. A single person will get a tailor to sew them four to five, even six uniforms to dress up on one occasion.

Celebrating birthdays is okay and normal. It is an occasion to be grateful to God Almighty for His blessings on every one of us. It is necessary to be thankful for being more mature, successful, famous, healthier, etc., than the previous year. Many of us do it every year, are happy to live another year and receive good wishes from family members, friends, fellows, etc. Nowadays, even birthday parties are labeled "mondial". There is no such thing as a "mondial" birthday, though. Do people realize one is getting closer to death at every new birthday? People go on a spending spree, spending lavishly a lot of fortune on things for a birthday party is some of the most outlandish things in the world. But that is what happens and what is witnessed repeatedly nowadays throughout the day. Some birthday parties look like the wedding ceremony of some rich guy who just got a fortune by winning a jackpot on the latest lottery. The birthday parties are held either at an expensive restaurant or hotel or at a park with delicious dishes ordered from one of the most excellent restaurants in the city. You see some of them donning the newest styles of clothes and looking attractive and pretty as hell. These parties take four to five hours, some half a day and others an entire day. It does not matter if it lands on a weekend or a weekday. On weekdays, they call in sick and go on their adventure.

Be it a "mondial" wedding ceremony or a "mondial" birthday party, it is noticeable that these people buy things they do not need to impress people they do not like. They spend their money because society, friends, or families want them to do it. They sometimes buy things that do not make them happy but because they make others happy. They buy things to impress other people. Very few people (countable on the fingers of one hand) will always stay faithful and loyal to you for doing such a thing.

I was brought up to bet on myself and be frugal. Dad and Mom never condone wasting things, anything. They were cautious and warned us not to take things for granted. They told us to take good care of our possessions, natural resources, and living and nonliving beings. Mom especially seemed more concerned about wasting things and warned us when she saw we took things for granted. She always had a watchful eye on our food use, water use, money use, etc. She never let us eat more than we needed. She would always say that eating more than you need is wasting food, is dangerous for health and is a sin. We usually had to eat the heated leftovers of the previous night's dinner for breakfast. So, is using water purposeless? She would say, "A lot of people out there do not have water or have to travel long distances to get water, so we have to be careful every time we want to use water."

We were not allowed to take multiple showers and had to wait until we had enough dirty clothes to wash on laundry day. My parents both grew up in the highlands and traveled there regularly after moving to the lowlands. They had witnessed people walking down the hills to fetch water from the wells and carry it up the mountain to use it for all purposes. When it came to money, Mom has always been strict. I got only what I needed. We only sometimes receive big money from our parents to treat ourselves with snacks, sweets, etc., daily.

Mom was willing to buy toys for me only if they were quality and long-lasting. She never agreed to buy me toy guns because, for her, they were always associated with violence. She said, "Toy guns would harden your heart and make you vulnerable to use real guns easily further down the road."

Mom gave me money only once a week in primary school on market days. For the rest of the week, she ensured we had enough food for the family. According to the birth order, she would give us different amounts on market days. The older one was, the more money one would get. The difference is a little. The older would get ten, fifteen, or twenty-five francs CFA more than the younger. The maximum difference the older would benefit from was twenty-five cents.

I had ten to fifteen francs CFA weekly on snack and market days. Every market day, she looked me in the eyes and said: "here is your snack money; choose carefully what you need for a snack."

During the school year in my primary school schooling, Mom rarely gave me money to take to school. She made sure I ate enough food before leaving. If I were going to be late for school, she would put some snacks in my bag to take with me to school. She would get the snacks from the snacks she made for her incoming generating activities, such as the African locust beans, crash ground peas, etc.

I learned to save money instead of spending on things just for the sake of spending it. As I grew older, I held the money I received from my parents and siblings on special occasions. When my brother Daniel visited us from Cote d'Ivoire, where he lived with his family, he told me to keep the changes after he sent me to get something from the shopkeeper. The following year, my brother Daniel revisited us during the same period, and I had the same amount of money kept under my Mom's suitcase. In middle school, I made about one thousand and five hundred francs CFA from selling millet and groundnuts that I gleaned from the leftover harvest. I kept it in my wallet for as long as I could remember. My friend, the principal's brother, Adama, told everyone I would never spend that money. He funnily persuaded people, "Since I met him, he had the same amount with him in his wallet."

I only took the wallet out of my pocket while sleeping in my room. Mom had put in my habits to spend when needed only. Since I did not need to spend money, it stayed with me all the time.

It is shocking to see people financially struggling to spend money on needless things during social events such as birthdays and wedding ceremonies and call them "mondial" events. I learned through experience that life is built step by step and level by level, patiently until one attains breakthrough and natural growth. True breakthroughs and real change cannot just happen by waving a magic wand. Many do not know what it takes to be a self-made millionaire or billionaire. My best friend Kernan Bagley used to say, "It is like working eighty hours a week for twenty to thirty, even forty years, in a skill that you are excellent at."

Thanks to my upbringing and takeaway from experienced people, I have realized that everyone is different, and we were all born with different sets of cards. Some were handed life as a gift on a golden plate, and some were born with nothing or barely anything. I was born with little to nothing. I have learned that our sole responsibility is to knit together an effective and efficient life craftily. I grew up with the mindset that the life we long for is behind the wall of hardships and challenges that stand in front of us and the wall that we hate so much to climb over. We should stop expecting from other people or expecting things out of the blue and get to work and make things happen.

The key is to follow one course until success. It is to move towards a sole goal that you have set for yourself. It does not matter how slowly or fast you go. As long as you are moving in the right direction, you will get there. Snails' pace is really slow, but they get to their destination no matter how long it takes.

Mom constantly said: "Do not spend your money only aiming to impress people. People will judge you, whatever the situation, so do not live your life to impress them – live your life impressing yourself. Always stay true to yourself."

Here is what Mom bequeathed to me:

"Be frugal during a period in your life. Frugality is the key to the life we live in nowadays. You are never too young or too old to be frugal. Live below your means, at least for a while, as you put the pillars that sustain you deep in the ground. Do not spend all your paycheck or any other type of income all at once or on useless things. Build up an emergency fund you can fall back on in lean times. It will save you so much stress. Then, start working towards saving for the big goals in life, such as starting a business, building a house, getting another degree, getting married, etc. Once you get into the mindset of living below your means and saving as much as possible, you will be surprised at how much you can save up in a little/short time." Mom told me.

My American friend and father figure used to drop some jewels on me as well. He used to say this during my stay in the United States of America while I was mowing lawns with him. He wanted to ensure I was saving the money I earned from mowing grasses and remodeling houses, "If you save a dollar on every occasion, it will be a billion one day. It is better to have it and not need it than to need it and not have it. Live life on your terms, make your own decisions, weigh pieces of advice that you receive from people very carefully." He would insist on the management aspect. "Do you know what management means?" he would ask.

It is the act or art of managing all of your possessions.

He would then clarify, "Being good at management is getting the maximum out of the minimum you have, "So strive to increase your income and decrease your expenses." He believed and implemented the following statement, "when one plays the long-term games, one gets the long-term gains."

Dad cemented in me, "As a man, you have a lot on your plate; you are young, and the world is your oyster. Do not try to live a comfortable life right now, especially when you are young and physically fit when your body can endure a lot in terms of heat, cold, workload, etc. There will be plenty of time to have fun and live comfortably; that is when you start to age, and your body needs more care, rest, and a comfortable life. There will be plenty of time to dress up with the latest styles and make it there further down the road. You have to put the work and the learning in first. Work on the things that will get you good and positive results. Give value to learning and education over entertainment or playing."

Mom and Dad recommended reading at every opportunity, including the Holy Bible. Mom, in particular, said, "The scripture is the pillar that sustains you. It keeps your feet from tumbling and lightens your route. As a young man, you need to work hard. I mean, like, really hard. You cannot just stay around the house or be a couch potato. There are only three reasons for you to be seen in the house during the day. First, when nature calls, that is to sleep (wake up early in the morning) and chase the dream you had last night if you had one. If you do not have a dream, create one and go after it. Second of all, that is also when nature calls you. That is to use the bathroom, and the third of all, it is to pray. You need to be spending time with God. Bare those three moments, grapple with everything that will make you grow constantly. Have a laser-like focus on the most important goals of your life, be patient, and lay one brick at a time."

My host Mom also used to say, "Do not spend your time watching television. You can watch TV strategically to recharge, do not play video games, screw around with social media, and waste your valuable time."

"Keep busy doing your thing. Now, keeping busy and being always on the go will make you boring because you will have no time to spend with your friends and mates who sit in the streets doing nothing." She highlighted, "You will not have time to make tea or gossip with them while sitting on the corner of a street. However, you must avoid that to be successful and have a stable and modest life. You can make the right decision at the right time when you have priorities and are focused on reaching your objectives."

Dad never got tired of saying this, "Bet on yourself and control whatever is possible for you to be in control of. Leave what you cannot control because it is out of your hands anyway." Dad would order, "Get your life together and control everything controllable in your life." Control here equals reach as far as your means allow it. Any means, be it physical, emotional, intellectual, professional, mental, etc., controlling these abilities will take you far in life and will enable you to have success."

Yet, what I see when I look around me is contrary to how I was raised. I see young people with solid background, blossoming of confidence and fortitude, healthy, physically strong, handsome, well-built, light-skinned, dark-skinned, happy, smiling, proud, delightful, intelligent, thoughtful, full of energy and talent sitting by the roadside, in streets making tea, smoking cigarette or shisha unwilling to work.

I met Mister Coulibaly as a freshman at the university. I appreciated and still appreciate him just because he is upright. Throughout my short life, Mister Coulibaly is one of the most telling figures who had left marks on my personality. He is average in height but an ace in character, attitude, and conduct. I had already taken one class, "the improving conversation class," with him as a freshman. In my sophomore year, I was taking translation classes with him. These are classes that develop the learners' special and general translation skills.

One day, I was in the classroom using a recently purchased brand-new phone during class. Unexpectedly, my phone rang, and Mr. Coulibaly looked me in the eyes and said: "I hate telephones." I responded, "I am sorry, I am sorry." I was different than the type of student who used electronics in class. I knew the distractions caused by electronics and avoided their use as much as possible while in school, especially in class. On that day, I was caught off-guard by a classmate of mine. I had just purchased a brand-new phone, and some classmates were aware of it because they saw me with the phone a few minutes before class started. I was wearing the earpiece in the classroom, and a classmate dialed my number in the middle of the class. That prompted the professor, Mister Coulibaly, to make me aware of his horror for phones. But it is a lesson I learned well and contributed to my making.

Mister Coulibaly, who is of the Bamanan ethnic group, one day told me that in the culture of the Bamanan people, an ethnic group in Mali, it is known that a child from another family is not adopted or accepted in one's family. It is somebody else's child. There is a perfect reason why people refuse to welcome somebody else's child in their household. Bringing somebody else's child into one's household and educating and treating them and your children on equal footing is very difficult. Our human nature most often fails us to do so. We show impartiality in our way of doing things for them and offer them different attitudes in our conduct, speech, and looks.

So, we tend to ask somebody else's child to do the complicated tasks. We invite and expect them to do the physically strenuous job, the complex tasks, and the most difficult, the dirtiest, and the most dangerous tasks. We do our best to spare our children from these challenging tasks and activities. By doing this, we show our children love and save them from life's difficulties. At the same time, we forget that we are training somebody else's child to life skills and hardships. Before we realize it, it is too late. We have trained somebody else's child to be good at everything, at life's most important things. They become independent and start fending for themselves and can take care of themselves in every situation in life. They have become better than our children.

Bamako is an ever-busy city, a typical capital city. The traffic is ever congested and causes a lot of pollution. Nowadays, pollution is the biggest challenge. It is a challenge that each of us is facing.

Be it morning time, daytime, or nighttime, it does not matter when; it is just up there hanging in the air everywhere throughout the entire city and even in the suburbs. I am talking about road dust, exhaust fumes, waste burnings, industrial emissions, and solid fuels, like raw coal used for cooking food, heating water, and other drinks such as tea, coffee, etc. Road dusts are, in particular, the biggest issue in the city and around. It is a city where you have a nightmare wherever you park your car, motorbike, etc. When you return after finishing your eight-to-five or nine-to-five office work and walk out to drive home, you will find your vehicle soaked with road and street dust. As a delivery van driver, a cab driver, or a personnel chauffeur, you will drive around for two to three hours through the city, and the inside of your car will all be dusty. You would take your vehicle from the car wash to park in the garage, and a few hours later, it would be covered up with dust. You close the doors and windows of your house and keep them firmly tight, but that does not prevent these specks of dust from getting into your home. They are as aggressive as a teddy bear, as sharp as a tack, and as penetrating as a needle.

They get past even the tightly closed aluminum windows and doors, find their way to the living room and the bedroom, and cover up your dining table, your TV set, your wardrobe, your sofas, and armchairs, etc. when they cover furniture up; they stay glued like super glue. The fine dust named Particulate Matter (PM10, MP2.5, PM1, and PM0.1) gets into your bedroom and finds itself in the depths of the room and at the bottom of the wardrobe. Imagine how easily they can pass through our nostrils and enter our lungs. The fine specks of dust are caused primarily by road dust and engine exhausts. Everybody is choking it on, from motorists and cyclists to wheel-barrow pushers, rickshaw pullers, panhandlers, vendors, traffic regulators, etc. We are all exposed to it and breathe in and out of the toxic air daily. We roam the city and the suburbs without face masks or protection.

Rougeaud is a Moto-Taxi driver and is exposed to dust all day long every day.

His wife complained, "Every day is the same. He comes in every night with a different color."

She added that she washes his clothes every night so he can wear them the following day when he leaves the house for another ordeal. She laments that the cycle continues. She fears for him, his health, and his well-being, but what can she do? Nothing. She said her husband graduated from university a few years ago but could not land a white-collar job, so driving the Moto-Taxi is his top opportunity and perhaps the only one.

The dust pandemic is all over us. It is too dangerous a situation for older people and children in particular. That is why we constantly suffer from colds, coughing, and sneezing. That is why many of us have allergic symptoms. That is why asthmatic people suffer so much. That is why our clothes get dirty quickly. That is why we are all sick. All of us have some nagging health issues. You can see the haze at night near street lamp posts and cars' or motorbikes' headlights. Urgent action is needed from the authorities and the civilians alike. The government should take drastic measures to cut pollution and limit traffic, such as implementing an effective public transportation system allowing commuters to use less of their engines. In addition, the government should advise the population against buying and using older cars, which cause more exhaustion. It should construct more asphalted roads, more paved streets, etc. More measures to reduce burn-offs and road dust are needed. Civilians should drastically reduce unnecessary trips they take with their cars, motorbikes, etc. More walking and less driving are required. They should avoid, at all costs, burning leaves and trash regularly. Families need not buy two or three cars when one can do the trick. People should stop buying one motorbike for each child and buy one per two.

"Each unwise human choice has a ripple effect on the rest of humanity, and we cannot avoid that."

Growing up, I loved the environment in which I lived. I lived in the village in my childhood, breathing fresh and pure air all year. The town was very peaceful and enjoyable and had an amicable environment. A friendly and clean environment makes a healthy mind in a healthy body. As I continued my studies, I moved to bigger cities after bigger cities. At first, I thought these bigger cities were cleaner, fresher, and purer, but after moving in, I realized that the air was less clean, the streets were more littered in many locations, and the environment was less sound than in the village. People did not care much about sibling environments. Cities where there are supposedly more schooled people, more enlightened people, more intelligent people, more aware people, and more caring people. The bigger the city, the more crowded it is. With the crowd of people that live in cities, more cars are being driven, more fuel is being burned, more houses are being built with more water being used, and more food is being eaten, resulting in more garbage being thrown. In addition, the factories in big cities produce more waste.

It is a daily experience for city dwellers, visitors, and commuters. One witnesses on a typical day the negligent and careless conduct of human beings. It is the standard of life nowadays.

A Bentley is among the world's most expensive and sought-after car brands. In a developing country like mine, the owner of a Bentley car is up there in the world of the haves. Anybody who can afford a Bentley is supposed to know the importance of protection and care because this car needs a lot of care and security. A standard Bentley manufacturer warranty lasts a few years until the automobile needs repairs. It supports the fact that owners of this car need to put in a lot of effort to protect and take care of their car.

The owner of this Bentley understood that. His Bentley Bentayga was very clean and very well taken care of and had no exhaustion. One day, I drove to the bank and was kept there for a few hours before returning to the office. On my way back to the office, I saw a Bentley right in front of me in congested traffic downtown Bamako, on one of the busiest streets ever. It is called Alqode Street and goes past the front of the Gabriel TOURE Hospital. Anybody driving down this street knows how busy it can be on many days. There were a few people inside proudly seated while the chauffeur was on duty. The people inside did not seem too bright because they were loud and did not care much about what was happening in the traffic. In this stop-go, stop-go traffic, I noticed the car's back door slightly opening. As I was looking to see what would happen, I saw a half-full cup of coffee, a paper cup, being dropped on the road by one of the adults sitting in the car's back seat.

The cup dropped onto the floor, and the content spread all over the area, leaving a dark spot on the hot road floor. I could not believe my eyes at what I had just witnessed. The person slammed closed the car door and kept talking to the rest of the passengers as if nothing had just happened. The coffee cup got run over by me and the other drivers behind me. This person is not dumb; otherwise, he would have dropped the cup with the coffee inside the car, I guessed. He knew it would be a mess if he had dropped it in the car. So, he decided to pollute the environment. He perhaps would never realize the damage he had caused the environment by committing this crime. Yes, it is a crime. Many people do not mind taking good care of their belongings but do not have the guts to handle the common good, "sibling environment."

An Acura brand is also up there with the luxury cars in the world. An average earner in my country cannot afford to have an Acura and drive it regularly. It is not the type of cars like the Toyota or Mercedes that one can see around daily in the traffic. It is not any Acura but an RDX Premium Sport Crossover—the expensive one. The owner, at least, was a middle-class, if not an upper-class citizen. He is a successful entrepreneur. The owner was very much a family man. I saw him as a family man because he had two kids and teenagers in the car who looked like siblings. They all looked alike, and the sir behaved like a father figure to the siblings alongside him in the car. The sir seemed cleaned, well-groomed, and dressed with the rich bazin getzner. So well-dressed were the siblings. They were clean and well-bred.

On this day, I was driving home from my friend Amadomo Kassogue's house, as I do every Sunday afternoon. I have lunch with him and his wife, Marie Guirou, every Sunday at their apartment. While driving down the street in a popular neighborhood in the afternoon following the visit, I noticed that the passengers in the car were throwing plastic cups, wraps, and remains of the food, snacks, or whatever that they were enjoying in the car out of the slid down back windows on both sides of the vehicle. It is a well-off man, and his family is littering the street and hurting the environment. They did not bother because it was just usual stuff for them. Polluting the environment is just no big deal to them.

A Suziki Vitara Hybrid is also an expensive car in the context of my country. It is a decent car, less expensive than an Acura RDX or a Bentley. Anybody driving this type of car is believed to be able to live above an average person. It was almost lunch hour on a weekend, and many people were preparing to have lunch at a popular Senegalese restauran. I had already parked my car, turned the engine off, and was about to go to the restaurant. I soon realized that lunch was not quite ready and the restaurant was being cleaned. I stayed in the car to wait for a few minutes. While seated, I saw this car right in front of me. I read the writing on the back side windshield and inspected the plate number. The owner had parked it in front of the most prominent boutiques in the neighborhood, next to the restaurant, to make some purchases. The restaurant is known for its affordable dishes and its delicious food. The boutique belongs to the SIMPARA. The SIIMPARA are very successful boutique owners. Their boutiques are known to have all kinds of internationally and nationally manufactured products needed by a typical household, and they are popular throughout the capital city.

The busiest period of the boutique is generally in the late afternoon. The car's owner was a medium-height, dark-skinned man in his fifties who came out of the boutique accompanied by a shop assistant carrying his items in various bags. He was sucking at a smaller plastic bag containing a drink he had probably purchased in the boutique.

Approaching the car, he opened the trunk and signaled the shop assistant to put the items inside. He had emptied whatever he was sucking at and dropped the trash just right by the driver's door on the floor before he stepped into the car and drove away. Meanwhile, two young ladies at the Senegalese restaurant were cleaning the restaurant floor before it opened and letting clients in for lunch or food. They both wore a pink handkerchief around their heads. One of them had seen the entire scene and surreptitiously pointed towards the car while talking to her workmate. They both seemed flabbergasted by the act of a man of this caliber. They were probably disappointed but minded their business and continued cleaning the restaurant's floor. At least they were doing their best to have a sound environment in the restaurant for their clients.

It is also a city full of public vehicles and bikes. Many people use public transportation, but most people using this type of public transportation are blue-collar workers such as cleaners, cooks, guards, small income-generating workers, small shopkeepers, etc. The vehicles used for this purpose are generally vans manufactured in Germany one million years ago. It is a type of transportation that is the most common. The majority of the population cannot afford to own a car. They ride taxis regularly to work and do not have or like motorbikes. It can be precisely said that it is how the haves commute daily. These vehicles carry passengers from one part of the city to another all day. Some people riding in these vehicles are seen throwing trash (cans, bottles, plastic wrappers, and plastic bags) out of the windows. Even the lay people who are supposed to suffer much from the hardships and damage caused by pollution, such as rises in temperature, diseases, etc., do not care about protecting the sibling environment. Nobody cares about the environment. The haves-not do not care for the environment, and the haves do not. Daily, we all see and witness the pollution of the environment in broad daylight. The streets are littered with garbage, covered with indescribable filth. It is so shocking that one wonders what the future holds for all of us. People need to be accountable to their community. The authorities are not punishing us, but we must be responsible for their acts.

A diaper in our beloved street. A lady in her thirties undressed the young boy whom she had just come to get from his school. The boy is probably in pre-school. She threw the diaper around the corner of the street adjacent to the school on the floor. The lady was dressed with the latest style of women's garment, Wax Real, freshly sewn. It looked tight on her and was a good fit. Whoever did the sewing job is an expert. She had long, black, shiny hair tied up in a ponytail. She is gorgeous and attractive on the look. The school is a high-tech school and was only attended by children whose parents are well-off. I was sitting at an eatery of a female friend of mine, Bebe. When she redressed the young boy with a new set of clothes, she held his right hand, put his bag on her shoulder, and walked past me to the eatery. Bebe was also able to see what just happened.

"Did you see the disgusting act I just saw?" I asked her.

"It happened before everybody's eyes in this street," she said.

"This is incredible!" I shouted, "A well-dressed, fine, neat, and clean lady like this is not supposed to do that."

"She is well-dressed and looks fine, and clean does not mean that she will act properly in life, my friend," she murmured, "One's look is not a guarantee of one's environment."

"I am shell-shocked now; I cannot just understand how people pollute their environment like that," I said.

"It is you who see this as a crime or an offense. We are used to this every day of our life," she shrieked.

Even though the school has a garbage can, this lady always remembered collecting and putting the diapers in the garbage can. Looking at the lady, the standing of the school, and the means at her or her family's disposal, you would think she would naturally take care of the environment the way she takes care of herself. You would never believe she would do such a thing. Unfortunately, it is a typical case, and we are all responsible one way or the other. We don't care about the environment a bit.

Bebe was concerned by the look on her face.

I asked her, "Why are you so downcast?"

"I am apprehensive about my eatery business with many people like this lady behaving like this every day," She feared.

She thought her clients would stop coming to eat or buy her food if they saw diapers on the street regularly. I assured her that the school's owner would refrain from putting up with the parents of the first graders, preschoolers, or kindergarteners to continue dropping their garbage around.

Bebe cooks the healthiest, most delicious, and most affordable food in the neighborhood and beyond. She obtained her vegetable ingredients fresh from local gardeners and never owned a refrigerator or a freezer to keep her sauce or whatever remained from yesterday. She would go to the local market to buy the newest ingredients, like peanut butter, eggplants, peppers, onions, spinach, etc., as early as six in the morning. She would come back home one hour or later to start the cooking with the help of her sisters and the maiden.

From twelve-thirty, her food is ready and taken freshly from the stove to the eatery, where a couple of dozen people are waiting for her. Some of them have their lunch at the eatery, and others would order takeaways to have lunch at their places. Those who order takeaways are welders, mechanics, repairers, appliance sellers, mattress sellers, second-hand item sellers, etc. Some of them come from as far as five kilometers daily to get their share of the lunch delight. Occasionally, she would close the eatery for social events or national holidays, and her clients would be disappointed not to have her treats.

The next day, when she came, they would tell her, "Bebe, you betrayed us yesterday. We spent the day with an empty stomach, and please let us know when you will not show up next time."

"You leave that over there," shouted the older woman, "who do you think you are dropping them here?" Beware, young woman! Beware!

"No, I will leave them right here," responded the younger woman, "this is the street, not your house; everybody is leaving theirs here. It is only me you can single out," please let me alone.

"It is not your house either; it is the street and belongs to all of us," retorted the older woman. "Do you hear me?" asked the older woman. "Show a little loyalty to your beloved country, please," ordered the older woman.

"You are the only person who always complains," yelled the younger woman. "What's wrong with you? Everybody is doing it every day. You think you are cleaner and more hygienic than everyone else in this neighborhood. Please live and let people live," Ordered the younger woman.

"Are you happy living in this situation, this dirt?" Vehemently asked the older woman.

"I do not care," responded the younger woman. "Nobody cares about it except you, so why would I care? Why do you want to be out of step with the majority? You are swimming against the tide, Miss Perfect."

She turned around and walked back into the house from where she came out as she spoke, leaving the older woman in the street shaking her head in total dismay.

Two women shouting at each other about where not to leave the garbage. It is a city in which many people live in rental houses. Two-thirds of the entire population live in rented houses or apartments. Even the people who owned homes most of them inherited from their forebears, who were the first settlers in the neighborhoods. There are many such neighborhoods throughout the city. Many such communities are like dumpsters. The houses in these neighborhoods were built with mud and covered with sheet metal. They were built for extended families (households) with ten to twenty family members. Land planning could have been better because the plots came in different forms, sizes, and shapes. Many parts of these neighborhoods did not have sewers, and in areas with sewers, the sewers needed to be more significant to serve the needs of the inhabitants. The problem is that the people in these areas must do more to improve the issues. They are throwing trash everywhere. They throw their waste into the sewers. The sewers are full of litter, garbage, and waste. Some families have garbage areas in front of the house where the dwellers gather their trash, but the problem is that the garbage is heaped in there for days, weeks, and even months. It makes the surroundings smelly, polluted, and challenging to breathe.

How can we live in this filth and be healthy? How can we live in this situation and stay virus and gems-free? We are our downfall, looking at how we treat the environment around us. We know the consequences, but we choose to continue down the road that will lead to destruction. We better get our act together and collectively work for a more sustainable future. The most important thing is we should never take our existence for granted.

All human activity is changing the climate. Every mess we make impacts the environment, but we can do something about it. We do not want to finish our lives like the Neanderthals, who were extinct due to their lack of care for the environment they lived in. The Neanderthals did not know much about their downfall, but we humans are aware of our actions and where they will lead us.

What is good citizenship? Are the leaders the reflection of the citizens, or are the citizens the reflection of the leaders?

When the Covid-19 pandemic broke out in Mali, the country was still plagued with problems arising from the 2012 coup, which was caused by rebellion, an act of armed resistance and unrest, a state of dissatisfaction, disturbance, and agitation in the northern part of the country. The population in the regions of the north of Mali felt unhappy and complained about the lack of infrastructure and other means of development in the said regions, or so it appeared. Besides, there was something shady going on about the former colonizer, and civilians were accusing France of meddling with the country's political life.

During Covid-19, several countries, including major world powers, were shutting down businesses, education facilities, and government agencies, private enterprises, imposing curfews, and postponing significant events to keep social distancing and to respect the measure of barriers against the Covid-19 disease. The government in Mali was similar to such health-wise standards, except that it decided to maintain the election (the election of the members of the Parliaments). It was a significant protocol breach vis-à-vis the fight against Covid-19.

Following the two rounds of the elections and the announcement of the final results by the Mali Supreme Court, militants from some significant political party candidates started demonstrations in some districts in Bamako and the regional capitals such as Kayes and Sikasso, resulting in the pillage and burning of public property. Boys as young as thirteen and fourteen years old were seen in this city's streets and major roads burning worn-out tires and garbage cans full of garbage, blocking the streets and main roads.

During this week and the weeks following demonstrations, driving to work was very difficult because minor detours were needed to avoid the potholes, burned areas, and other damages caused to the roads. These militants, the demonstrators, accused the President of the Supreme Court of deliberately voiding some vote counts in some populated areas to favor the party in power. They were using profanities and obscenities towards the President of the Supreme Court. Some of them used all sorts of disgusting insults and treated the President of the Court as the one who caused trouble throughout the country. These critters also blocked the main roads and streets using hard rocks, worn-out tires, and cement bricks to prevent police officers from driving their pick-ups on the roads and dispersing them.

As a result, policemen were driving them away by throwing tear gases and shooting in the air. One night, I was lying on the rooftop to sleep peacefully and was enjoying the natural flow of fresh air. Sleeping inside was very difficult and uncomfortable due to the enormous heat in the dry season from March to May. From the rooftop, I stood up and witnessed with my very eyes teenagers and young men in their twenties showing their dissatisfaction and unhappiness both at the final results of the MP's election and the imposition of the curfews (as a safe measure regarding the Covid-19) which kept night workers such as bartenders, night club owners, grilled meat sellers, bar owners, etc. indoors, preventing them from making money that they live on. Many of the population was fed up with the lax measures regarding Covid-19. Yes, flexible criteria because while the government maintained curfew, le Grand Marché de Bamako was open, people kept organizing wedding ceremonies and attending burial ceremonies in masses. That is despite the government's firm decision to avoid gatherings and get-togethers of more than fifty people once and in a location.

The expression Mali Koura (New Mali) became very popular in the year 2020s. Demonstrators were heard saying it during the series of demonstrations staged by the M5-RFP (Mouvement du 5 Juin - Rassemblemt des Force Patriotiques) against the regime of the former and late President Ibrahim Boubacar KEITA, who was later overthrown in the same year two thousand and twenty-two. *Mali Kura* means *New* Mali, a Mali that detaches itself from its old self. According to its proponents, the Mali Koura era is a new one that will do away with all that is harmful to its progress, development, and the nation's success. Mali has been wrought with corruption, injustice, violence, conflicts, and bribery in the last few decades, and the country has gone through multiple coups since it became independent. A country that has seen about and experienced everything unwished in a country's being: the Mali Koura is an ideology and a desire to have a peaceful country where it feels good to live, with harmony, justice, mutual respect, and solidarity and hospitality.

We call ourselves good citizens; we all point our fingers at someone else. It reminds me of the adage: "Charity begins at home and justice next door." It is someone else's fault if injustice, corruption, embezzlement, and the environment are so filthy. The atmosphere is so filthy and smelly because the other is not doing the right thing. As a citizen, I am not doing the right thing, and that is fine because it is only me, and I have the right to do so. As a citizen, I will only do the right thing if people do the right thing. In some smelly parts of the city, one must hold their breath while walking, driving, or riding by. We accuse the government, the authorities, the rulers, the mayors, etc., but we behave as disobedient and as unlawfully as we can every day, all day long. How can we expect the authorities that we have chosen, who eat the same food that we eat, drink the same water that we drink, breathe the same air that we breathe, have the same ambitions, and we want them to be an angel or have a different nature, sent from heaven. We do not protect our rivers and other water bodies. We put our wastes and garbage into these waters, harming and killing water species. We fish the same water species, use them as food, and expect to be healthy. We do not sweep our door front and our street. We take the garbage outside and drop it in front of the door and on the street. Imagine every single family cleaning the front of their door. The city will be clean and will be a haven. But nobody cares; as long as it is not in my sleeping space, I am fine.

We are living and witnessing these:

As a citizen, you run into the red light, deliberately drive or ride the wrong way, hit someone in the traffic, and run away. You do not pay the road taxes for your car and motorbike, but that is fine. At the same time, you complain that the roads are full of potholes. You pull up your vehicle by the roadside while half of the car is on the road and the other half on the other side, blocking the free flow of traffic, preventing road users from minding their business, and still pretending to be worried about traffic accidents and road rages. Good citizens drive or ride to the traffic lights at midnight, probably the less busy traffic time, and stop there when no car or motorbike is coming on the left or right until the light is green. As a citizen, you steal power by rigging the electricity meter and refusing to pay bills but still want the country's development. As a citizen, you steal tap water, do not pay the bill, and still expect the country to be able to provide safe drinking water to everyone. As a parent, you bribe a school owner or pay a teacher money to have your child pass to the superior class. As a teacher, you accept bribes to allow a pupil/student to pass to the next level. As a student, you copy from your neighbor and cheat in class to be successful in your exams and tests. As a businessman, you refuse to pay taxes or cheat on the right amount to be paid. As a tax collector, you use the taxpayers' money for your vested interest.

As a shopkeeper, you sell your product the wrong amount at the regular price. You sell less than a kilogram at a kilogram price, you sell less than a liter at a liter price, and you are fine by the judgment of your conscience. As an employer, you are okay with being bribed all day to give employment to those who do not deserve the position simply because you cannot control your greediness. You hire the wrong person to perform a job he/she is not qualified for. As a judge, you rule on a fraudulent narrative. You knowingly and wrongly pronounce judgment on the innocent, condemn them, and put them into prison because you got a visit from one party the previous night. Justice is lost in plain sight.

As a singer, you need a sense of morale/ethics. As a religious person, you have no intention of divinity. As an entrepreneur, you treat your employees as enslaved people, but you say you want them to make breakthroughs and succeed in their jobs or careers. You do not even pay the minimum wage to some workers. You are forging the figure of your revenue to spend less on taxes. As a doctor, you make surgery for a disease that never existed to charge money to the so-called sick. You make people lose their lives because you have little knowledge. You prescribe medication and direct the so-called patients to your friend who has a drugstore and later claim your share/benefit for sending patients with prescriptions to his pharmacy. As a teller at a bank, you assimilate forged banknotes with real ones. You call yourself a good citizen, but you never bother to embezzle money in your organization destined for the vulnerable, the destitute, and the needy. As an upper-class citizen, you live in a neighborhood where people live below the poverty threshold. Some are in abject poverty; they cannot even afford the three meals of the day, and you advocate for them as an executive in your Caritas organization or your association to fight against poverty. You have a good life, a cushy job, and live comfortably. Still, you are jealous of the breakthroughs of the young trainees, the new graduates, the less fortunate, and the soon-to-be entrepreneurs and pin them down.

Strangely and ironically enough, these people talk incessantly about and want the much coveted *Mali Koura*.

The Ones Who Prey On the Weak The Ones Who Prey On the Weak

As a policeman/woman, you wrongly arrest people and make them pay money without issuing a ticket. You receive money from a thousand people erroneously and illegally and use it for yourself. The worst thing is when you stop some people because they did not pay tax for their engines, but they bribe you to let them go, and you are happy because you get the illegal money. You need to remember your primary purpose: to help road users in the traffic and help them be safe.

This case happened on a hot, rainy summer afternoon in congested traffic leading the way to the airport in the capital city of Bamako. It was unfortunate because I had just left the burial ceremony of one of my church member's sons, who transitioned a few days ago. The deceased was so young. He passed away in his early twenties. It was an unfortunate afternoon, and you could read it on the faces of everyone who had attended the burial.

"Peeep! Peeep! Please, sir, I need the car registration document," Said the policeman.

I was driving home from the funeral with my friend's and brother's wives, who were nursing a baby. She had left her baby boy home for a couple of hours to attend the burial ceremony. I was giving them a ride home, and a policeman pulled us over at a traffic light. He made me stop the car in the middle of the heavy traffic and ordered me to give him the car registration document, which I did because I thought it was a routine and random check because the country was in turmoil.

Terrorists had attacked the city of Bamako a few days ago. But this was neither a routine nor a random check. Surprisingly, the policeman accused me of running into a red light. The ladies in the car could not believe their eyes and ears. This policeman stood beyond the traffic lights and could not tell if the traffic lights were green, yellow, or red. Everything happened before their own eyes. After he had stopped us, the motorists behind us on the second lane drove past me without him or his colleague, who was sitting on his bike, stopping them. I told myself he had seen something unfamiliar with my small car, so he pulled me over. I had to pull the car on the side of the road to free up some space to enable the motorists behind me to pass. After pulling up the car, I approached the policeman to recover the registration documentation. The ladies in the car got out to follow me to let him know he was wrong in stopping me for something that did not happen.

At that time, he had already stopped another older motorist behind a Mercedes One Hundred and Ninety Wheels on the same account and requested him to pay two thousand francs CFA. The older man was adamant; he disagreed and said it was a false accusation. The policeman would not listen to him and ordered him to pay. The older man swore in Allah's name that he did not run into the red light, but if the policeman wanted him to pay after he had tried his best to convince him that he was being robbed, he would pay.

Meanwhile, the policeman had ordered the ladies in my car to return to the car. At the same time, the other policeman was still sitting on his motorbike, watching the busy two-way traffic. Some of his victims, mostly Moto-taxi drivers, begged him to let them go, but he would not listen. He ignored them all together.

Back to the situation between the older man and the other police agent. The older man had taken out 10,000 Francs CFA (about twenty dollars) that he handed to the policeman, but he declined because he had no change and told the older man to find a solution to make the change and bring him the two thousand he asked for. So, the older man walked up to the nearest shopkeeper to buy some stuff that he did not probably need to buy to have some change. He returned to hand a two thousand francs CFA banknote to the policeman to recover his car registration document and left cursing and saying he was robbed of his money and that the cop was a crook. At this point, I was so angry that I started talking non-stop.

"What is the take on the acts of people? It is the Mali Koura that you are talking about and dreaming of. You are robbing your people in broad daylight. Do you have any idea of what you are doing?"

All the people who had been stopped were standing around and listening to my rant.

"You see this?" I asked.

I spoke: "People like this policeman are the ones who die on one of those days without being sick or injured. His people would then say he was good, nice, and kind. These are the types of people when karma hits them, and they suffer in life, his relatives are the ones who would say he was a good citizen . He did not deserve what happened to him; he served people and had the good of this country in his heart. But in reality, what he does every day when he leaves his family to go to work is to rob people and deprive them of their assets all day long. You will end up miserable. It irks me whenever I see these kinds of situations."

I kept telling him that I did not run into the red light, that the ladies in my car were eyewitnesses, and that he should return my car registration document. I did not intend to pay for a wrong I did not do. Since onlookers were looking at us and listening to what I said about crooked policemen. He came up to me, gave me back the car registration document, and asked me to leave if I was sure I did not run into the red light.

I took it and returned to the car while the standing-by onlookers were shocked by what was unfolding. I bet some were amazed at how I handled things with them. When people get stopped by policemen, they tend to beg or accept to pay the amount charged without trying or justification.

The private company I worked for planned a work session to implement its strategic plan for the next five years in another city located about three scores of kilometers away from the capital city, Bamako. Most staff had to travel there to work on the strategic plan. We left in the morning in October on a bright Saturday. This trip was the first of its kind, and the company had decided to bond purposes between the personnel. Working together in a new environment could generate positive outcomes for the staff members.

We were excited about the trip; it was our first time carpooling as colleagues. There were two cars: A Prado Toyota belonging to the Director General of the company, Mister Sidibe, and a Kia belonging to the company's accountant, Mrs. Camara. Both cars were recently purchased and were in excellent shape. The Prado Toyota was recently delivered from the factory. We drove for about forty-five minutes before we started seeing the outskirts of the city we were going to. At the roundabout, before entering the gate to the town we were heading for, we got pulled over (the Prado) by a few police agents, claiming they were doing a routine check. At first, we thought they would finish the regular check in a few minutes, but that was never the case. One of the policemen came up and said that the two small back windows were tinted and that he could not let us drive into the city. None of us could believe our ears. The director general was sitting in the back seat and came out and talked politely to the policemen to convince them that his car was delivered from a factory in this state. They responded that they understood the car was delivered from the factory but insisted he still needed to pay money for keeping the tinted windows on.

One of the policemen started to speak out loud and was lecturing us. That is when things started to go off the rails. Most of us expected to hear a simple warning, but that was not to be. The policemen wanted to be paid some bride, which did not go well with the director general, who went up the wall. The director general even got more irritated when he discovered that the policemen themselves had tinted windows vehicles parked a few yards away from us under the big tree. They took away the car registration document from us and issued a handwritten ticket that we had to present to the chief of the police at the local police station downtown.

While driving towards the city center, one waved us to stop. We stopped, and a few of us walked over to him to listen to what he had to offer. He wanted to negotiate with us to pay a bribe instead of driving downtown to the chief officer to deal with the issue and return to recover the document. I believed he knew that letting us drive to the headquarters to pay and get the ticket would get the money paid into the state account. He did not explicitly ask for cash, but we all could see that he stopped us for the second time to convince us to pay without proof to use the money for himself. One of us, Mr. Keita, known for his frankness, joined Mr. Sidibe and said aloud that he would prefer to pay more money at the police station, which goes into the state budget. We all agreed that it was the right thing to do. So we decided to take the drive to the headquarters. When we arrived, we found a small stature man sitting in a tiny, cramped office. He wore glasses and had whitish underwear inside a blue t-shirt, the police uniform.

The director general was furious then, and his breathing rhythm was so fast. As soon as he faced the chief officer and started to talk, he lost control. Before he could gather, the policeman cut him off and told him to beware of this speech. He ordered him to pay 15.000 F CFA for what he labeled as a "breach." They could not understand each other, and the director took out the amount, five thousand and ten thousand banknotes, and threw them on top of his desk, but they fell onto the floor. He quickly picked up the banknotes on the floor and issued a ticket. We left his office to recover the vehicle registration document before heading for our work session around noon.

A few months after I witnessed the unfortunate event with the police on the road, the government of Mali initiated a process to manufacture a new card replacing the National ID Card called the biometric ID Card. The government created a website to allow citizens to validate their identification information using the data from the National Identification Number (NINA) online. The government also requested the population to register at the nearest Police Station or any other location where the registration can be done throughout the capital and upcountry. Registration at these locations is the main problem, especially at the police stations. It is a real headache for both the population and the police. The people already suffered from the problems of issuing National ID cards in the last few decades. It was always a headache to get one. One had to wake up as early as five in the morning to travel to the police station to be among the first fifteen or twenty people to get one issued to them. The police authorities never allocated more than fifteen to twenty IDs per day. The issuance of only a limited number of IDs was related to the limited number of available cards. People, having no choice, accepted the claim made by the police regarding the lack of cards. When the government initiated the process for the Biometric ID card, the population was initially relieved that it would be the end of their ordeal concerning National IDs. Still, it turned out to be quite the opposite. To be registered for the Biometric ID, one has to get as early as 1 a.m. or two in the morning to be among the first on the list, the first come, first served list. In the third week of January 2023, on a Tuesday, I woke up at five to rally at a police station in a popular neighborhood to get registered.

When I arrived, it was dark, and looking from my car window, I could see a few people sitting under a shelter in front of the police station. I greeted them and asked for the list. I was directed toward a man in his forties with a sheet in his hand.

"Can I write down my name, please?" I asked.

"What list do you need? The one to be issued a new national ID or the one for biometric card registration?" He asked.

"I am here to register for the biometric card," I replied.

"You cannot write your name on that list anymore," he said with a sorry voice.

"Why not?" I required.

"There is no more space to do that. I can only allow twenty people to write their names," He said.

"I am person number twenty-one; please let me write my name and try my luck if they do not accept that is it," I pleaded.

"Sorry, I was given clear instructions not to let anyone write their name after the twentieth person has written their name," he concluded.

But what is astonishing is that the police authorities decided to register only twenty people a day. I did my best to be on the list, but the instructions were no more names after the twenty-first people had written theirs. I stood there motionless for about ten minutes. I wondered why the police authorities register only twenty people daily when a hundred people can be registered a minimum daily! Fast forward to the second week of March 2023, I went for a haircut at my barber's, a friend of mine, Mister Seyndour.

He asked me, "Did you register for the biometric card?"

I said, "No, I did not. I tried a few weeks ago to do that, but I could not." I told him what happened that day.

He said, "I know someone doing the same thing the police are doing in the police station. I will put you two in touch."

I responded with amazement and happiness, "Really? Will he accept to do the registration for me?"

"He came over to my house to do for my wife and children the other day, and I do not see why he would refuse for a friend."

As he said, I had an appointment with mister SIDIBE at my Baber's the following week. Before the rendezvous, he had requested that I send him a picture of my passport so he could check and double-check my data. When he arrived at the shop fifteen minutes later, he took a mug shot and took my digital prints. He got me registered in less than five minutes.

I said, "Wow! Is this it?"

He responded, "Yes, you are all set."

"Why is this not the case in the police stations? I mean, they only take twenty people per day?" I wanted to know.

"I am also surprised, and I register as many as one hundred and sometimes more daily. When I collect the registration forms, I take as many as possible to use them for the next few days. After I return to collect more, I find that people are still using the forms they collected a few weeks ago," He regretted.

I mused the following: "There is a need for self-assessment. Self-assessment takes us into the nooks and crannies where we hide old grudges, secret hatreds, and bitter resentments. The development will not come from planet Triglon. It will not come down from the heavens, and even the angels cannot bring development here. Development will not come from Mars, Pluto, or other planets in our solar system. It will come from me and you. Change needs to come from us. We must put aside the vested interest and put forward the common good."

Charity Begins at Home and Justice Next Door

"There is a blockage in this street; there is no way to get in," said a cab driver behind the wheel of a Peugeot 306.

The street in this particular community had limited access to motorists, taxi drivers, and even ambulance vehicles in case of an emergency. There were no roadwork signs; some cement bricks and pieces of wood blocked the streets. Some motorcyclists could sneak if they ignored the danger of hitting a brick or firewood here and there. But something was going on somewhere down the road. It is a street that people used regularly to get to the other side of the city and was very solicited and needed by dwellers who lived on the other side. With the blocked street, the dwellers who commuted downtown had to take a long detour to reach their homes. Two middle-aged women, a dark-skinned taller and a light-skinned shorter woman, were sitting on the edge of the blocked street facing a rental house, talking to each other. The older lady with the lighter skin was selling condiments on a three-legged table covered with a blue tablecloth on which she spread her vegetables. The rental house seemed very animated and very busy. Younger women and teenagers wearing uniforms and make-up were pacing up and down the other side of the blocked streets. Some of them seemed very upbeat about something going on in their life. Others were taking selfies and shooting photos and were in high heels. An event was happening inside the rental house or the two-level building facing the rental house.

Loud music was heard from the corner down the street, to which some children were excitedly dancing. The two middle-aged women were still talking and disagreeing about the blocked road. The shorter woman was nursing a toddler. The toddler was excited about seeing the dancing children fifteen yards away. He was so excited that he started to dance while sucking at his Mom's breasts. "Enough," said his Mom, pushing him away, gesturing jokingly, "Go dance with the others." The women were looking at the drivers and motorists, unaware of the road blockage coming, and turning around to go back from where they came from irritated.

The driver of the Peugeot 406 was still stranded in the street, unable to turn around swiftly because of the traffic behind him. The driver, a short man in his forties, was sweating hard behind the wheels. He sweat so much that he used the back of his hand to wipe the sweat away from his forehead. He was chuntering about the mess being caused around the street and seemed to condemn the culprit. Finally, the taller, dark-skinned woman spoke up. She spoke loud enough so people in her vicinity could hear.

"This is not fair; it is not right," she said, "look at the number of cars down the streets. It has paralyzed an entire neighborhood, and it is getting worse. A lot of people are suffering in this traffic jam. All because of a wedding ceremony."

Yes, this street is being blocked for a wedding ceremony being held down there. Meanwhile, a nineteen-year-old lady was walking down the next street with a younger boy, probably her sibling, by her side.

The young lady responded to the woman, "That is alright, it is our "mondial" wedding! she hollered at the woman, "Road users can cope with that today, can't they? It is only today." She added, "We do not want motorists and cab drivers disturbing us with engine noises and honking."

They walked down the street joyfully to join another group of younger people dressed up for the occasion.

Watching all these actions was an older man in his seventies sitting under the ficus tree on a mat with his radio in his hand. I was sitting a few meters on his right side. I always sat by his side on weekdays and afternoons when I returned home from the office or on weekends in the morning or during the day. Before sitting by his side and starting conversations, I would greet him while kneeling and shaking his hands. I would ask how his day was, and he would do the same. He would end the greetings by saying his blessings, and I would say "Amen" and thank him for the blessings. I learned a lot every time I sat by his side. Based on what I heard in smaller classes about the quotation of a Malian intellectual and writer, Amadou Hampâté Bâ, who said: "In Africa, the death of an old man is like a library burning down." So, I seized every opportunity to listen to him.

That day, a Sunday, we observed and listened to all that happened with our very eyes and ears. He cleared his throat and corroborated what the women were saying about the blockage of the street.

"We are now living in a topsy-turvy society. It has lost its values, customs, and ideologies; everything is allowed without consequences," he regretted.

"Do you see what I am seeing and are angered by this?" I asked.

He stroked his white beard like a small and delicate animal, "Every day, you see new and weird things."

Showing his feelings, he said, "We, the elders, it is challenging to see and accept what we are witnessing daily, all day long. This younger generation is struggling a lot. They think they are all smart but only see things from one side. They think they have the freedom to do whatever they want. They are not aware that they are preventing others from having their freedom and peace by blocking the street. That is how smart they are! They think they are allowed to do anything without consequence and punishment. This street-blocking thing is widespread throughout the city and even the country. Blocking the streets has become a normal trend for every occasion, whether for a wedding ceremony, a naming ceremony, or any other event. It is why society seems to go from bad to worse for us baby boomers and Generation Ex. At this rate, the future does not look bright. It is a real crisis, and we are all aware of it. We live in a broken world. We try to treat the symptoms by large social programs and policies, but they can only do so little; they cannot tackle the society's problems from the source/bottom. We can only pray and hope for the best."

"Do we have any hope?" I looked at him.

"If we return to the old way of educating the children who are the future of this country, then yes!" he said pessimistically.

The old man told me, "A few days ago, I was sitting here, and a man approached to greet me in the nicest ways."

I said, "That was quite kind of him."

"Only for a moment," he said, "He wanted me to help him change his ten thousand francs CFA."

I said alright, "Were you able to help him out?"

"Yes," he said, "I more than helped him."

"Oh, that is nice of you," I complimented him.

"The young man was a crook; the ten thousand banknotes he gave me in exchange for the change was forged," he regretted.

I was speechless!

I told him I had a story to say to him, too. One day, I was sitting in the living room of my apartment in the early afternoon and heard someone knocking at my door. I came to open the door, and a soldier man was standing in his military lattice.

He asked, "Can I get in?"

"Yes!" I answered.

He came in and sat down without me giving him a seat. As soon as he sat, he started crying uncontrollably and said he had lost his parents this morning in Sevare. Sevare is located in the fifth region, about 700 kilometers from Bamako, the capital city.

He said, "I need money to attend their burial ceremony the following day."

I was so touched looking at him pained like that.

I told him, "I spent three years in Sevare when I was going to high school and have friends and classmates in the military camp, and I genuinely want to help, but I want to know more."

If anything, I would know about his parents, so I asked, "Which family in the camp are you from?"

At this point, he stopped crying but could not answer my question. He knocked at the wrong door. He was exposed. He was a crook and was deceiving people to give him money through this strategy. I kindly asked him to leave. He stood up and left. The older man just shook his head.

A few weeks later, a baby mama knocked at my door while I was napping. I approached the door, and she stood with a baby boy at her back.

She said, "Benjamin, good afternoon!"

I was surprised she called me by my name.

"Do you know who I am?" I inquired.

She said, "Yes!" "I always say hi when I see you sitting on the terrace while walking down the street. Don't you remember my face?"

"No," I said.

"This is my baby boy; he needs medical attention," She said.

"What kind of treatment does he need?" I asked.

She said with emotion, "He has a lot of pain when peeing; he needs to be circumcised."

I looked at the baby boy and felt for him.

I told her, "Can you come tomorrow."

And she said, "Yes."

After she left, I called an acquaintance to ask for a doctor available to circumcise a baby. He gave me the contact of the doctor, and I phoned the doctor and explained to him the situation. He said he could do the job, and we agreed on the price.

The next day, she showed up, and I told her, "I have found a doctor who can circumcise and heal your baby."

She looked a bit perplexed, "Alright, no problems."

I was thrilled because I would be helpful to someone.

I told her, "Bring the baby in a couple of days, and I will accompany you to the doctor's office." She agreed and said goodbye to each other, on the agreement that we would meet in a couple of days.

Guess what, she never came back. Later, I was told that she was a deceiver. She makes money off people doing these shenanigans.

"This is all lack of proper education," regretted the old man.

The old man genuinely believed family is where all is rooted, "Parents should do better in giving a worthy upbringing. Parents should ensure that when their children leave the house, they behave in a way that honors their names and brings them a good reputation. They should do their best to educate their children to become good citizens who put the nation's interest first." Recommended the older man.

"Do you believe parents can do that today? Do you think they have time to do that?"

"Look, it is all about commitment and putting in the efforts," he said, "Without those commitments and efforts, there is no way to do it."

According to him, the schooling is not up to part,

"I wonder what our educational institutions are doing. Schools were created to bring a new order of things. Education is supposed to bring harmony into our society, but we face new daily challenges. Our children, grandchildren, and great-grandchildren are getting away from our values, customs, and ideologies. They are just slipping through our fingers," wondered the old man.

"Are you disappointed with our schools," I asked.

"Of course I am; schools are failing in many ways nowadays," he moped.

I shared with him what I learned at Portland State University regarding the education we need and how we need to invest in the field of education.

People have different perspectives on education, "What is education for? Nowadays, the top priority of being educated is to have more things, different things, and better things than others.

The goal of education should be to transform the soul of the learner. It makes the learner wiser and more knowledgeable about the common good. The purpose of attending school is more than obtaining a degree or a better job. Education should be the driving force that eliminates competition among individuals in a given nation. Education should enable us to go beyond winners and losers (competing with each other and building success upon others' failures) and beyond the idea of better people and worse people.

The overarching goal of education should be something other than the pursuit of a prestigious career, personal wealth and independence, and material security. Still, it should be to educate global citizens who strive to establish harmonious relationships among human beings with the natural systems and other living and non-living beings.

In other words, schools should produce graduates who can move seamlessly from theory to practice and comprehend the relationship between human behaviors, beliefs, and natural systems. Graduates who have problem-solving skills about real-world sustainability problems and challenges. Graduates who have vital competencies to be "problem solvers," "change agents," and "transition managers." Those who fight to make this world a better place. Education should promote sustainable development. According to the document "Our Common Future" of the World Commission on Environment and Development (Brundtland Report), "Sustainable Development is a development that meets the needs of present without compromising future generations to meet their own needs." The well-being of both current and future generations depends solely on the current generation's lifestyles. Therefore, the lifestyles of individuals with ethical reasoning and action, intergenerational skills, and responsible citizens of their community are needed.

Invest in education, invest in teacher preparation purposefully. Education is the pillar of the development of any nation. The better-off countries have the best educational systems. Education has been genuinely funded in countries such as Singapore, Finland, and South Korea. In South Korea, the mantra is "Don't even step on the shadow of a teacher." In South Korea, the school system promotes a sense of loyalty and legitimacy to the state while promoting liberal democratic values linked with the state's close dependency on the USA. Korean parents have an obsession with giving their children top-rated education. South Korean mothers are nicknamed "Tiger Moms" because of their commitment and determination to secure decent education for their children. These countries turned the situation around from the ground up in a time as short as three decades. These countries have done away with endless strikes, negotiations, and bureaucracy regarding educational issues. Their climb from rock bottom to the top of the PISA and OECD ranking was achieved thanks to two distinctive features: the egalitarian ideal and the zeal for education (Linda Darling Hammond, 2010).

I shared with the older man that the egalitarian ideal favors providing the same educational opportunities and the same quality of education to all individuals, regardless of their race, gender, religion, sexual orientation, ethnic group, geographic and socioeconomic background. Learners should get the same quality of education; they should be treated the same by teachers and considered equals.

I hopelessly asked him, "Can we dream about the egalitarian ideal?"

"I hope we can achieve that; only by achieving the egalitarian ideal will we be able to have a stable society," guaranteed the old man.

I learned that the zeal for education is about placing a high value on education. Education should be the top priority of any individual, community, state, and nation. Education is a gateway to equality. It is the pipeline that leads to justice and peace. The drive for education transforms a country from impoverished to prosperous. It will play a significant role in building a more democratic society based on active citizen involvement in public affairs. In the United States, some parents homeschool their children. It is called "Homeschooling," a type of education parents undertake to educate their children at home. It is legal in all fifty states.

During homeschooling, the most important thing parents can offer their children is "to *like* them, enjoy their company, physical presence, energy, foolishness, and passion. In South Korea, parents' high value on education has enabled their children to obtain state-of-the-art education. I hope my country can emulate these countries." I said.

He genuinely hoped this would help us escape our country's current situation. I said, "I am in the field of education, but I do not see that zeal daily."

"It is another dimension we need to add to our educational system," he added.

Teaching is the mother of all professions. Teaching is an art. I told him for that to happen, "Teachers should teach to transform the essence of the learner to interact with the world and one another. They should educate learners as problem solvers, change agents, and transition managers. Learners who will become well-rounded citizens. Citizens who 'think globally and act locally."

Teachers are responsible for molding young minds. Therefore, all teachers must prepare learners for the future and understand that every learner is sacred, deserves fair treatment, and that all learners are respected and valued. Teachers are called to inspire learners to reach their full potential, be creative and innovative, and have both (written and oral) communication skills. As a teacher, you should accept and love your learners regardless of whether they are short, tall, thick, skinny, poor, rich, clean, or dirty clothed (Dr. Terrell L. Strayhorn, Ohio State University.)

In the long run, a teacher's success does not depend on his/her seniority, status, experience, and wealth; it depends on the accomplishments of those he/she taught and how his/her teaching, guidance, and nurturing changed the learner's soul. How he/she transformed them into change agents, problem solvers, and transition managers who have self-limitation for the sake of future generations."

He responded, "That is wonderful if we can afford that."

He said, "Let's educate hard-working, smart young people determined to beat the odds and make a difference. People who are educated are the most likely to have a better understanding of other people, better relationships with other people, a better spirit, a better common sense, and most importantly, better health."

He concluded, "What about thinking globally and acting locally? That will bring the new order beings into existence. I do not know how far that is, but that is the state needed."

"It seems too good to be true what you are trying to say, dear father. I pray and hope this happens while putting the work in myself as an educator."

After living in a particular community for several years, I moved to a new neighborhood called Missabougou. I enjoyed my stay one way or the other.

In this new community, there was a well-balanced man. He was a sports alcoholic. He has a quiet, conducive lifestyle in this community, one of Bamako's most peaceful and friendliest. He was active in the evening or early morning, working out in and around the neighborhood. He challenged the old saying, "An apple a day keeps the doctor away." It is one way of encouraging people to eat more fruit and vegetables frequently. According to the well-balanced slender man, thirty minutes of sport daily plus consuming fewer sugary drinks and salty, fatty, fast food keeps the doctor far away. The well-balanced slim man's experiences have proved that some disciplined sports activities keep one physically fit and mentally sharp and keep the doctor at bay.

Most people know the importance of sports and do something like walking, running, or pushups to level up their bodies. People try out sports activities in many ways. From walking to running, yoga to stretching, mountain climbing to cycling, rope jumping to pumping, or even pushups. People get involved in these sports activities for ten minutes, twenty minutes, an hour, and maybe more for others. Some of us do it for pleasure. Many others do it for health reasons when they are hit hard with diseases. In many cases, it is based on a recommendation given by a doctor.

The well-balanced man works out regularly nowadays, and every time he does, he stays in a particular sports activity for thirty minutes minimum. Before that, while growing up and during his studies, he used to play soccer or international football. But after he had graduated and obtained a cushy job, he stopped physical exercise altogether. Despite doing the job and being well-paid, he did not feel physically fit. He found his life a bit boring. He was having some issues concentrating on his work, and sometimes, his production needed to improve. He was occasionally hit by constipation and started sleeping disorders late at night. He struggled to fall asleep and used to wake up in the middle of the night.

He could remember that when he played football regularly, he passed out as soon as his head hit the pillows. Something inside him told him to return to his old habits, which was playing football. However, his work schedule prevented him from joining his mates with whom he could play football. So, he decided to jog, run, and stretch a few days a week. He regularly started to do these physical exercises fifteen years ago.

His objective in doing sport nowadays is to, first of all, stay slim, light, and have a lean body. Second, he wanted a flat stomach, shredded abs, six-pack abs, or whatever they call it.

He wanted a flat stomach by all means. Anything that makes him normal. "Anyone can have, do, and be just about anything they set their mind to." he guaranteed, "but you must be willing to pay the price to get it."

That is why the well-balanced, slender man resolved to do it. He was never a fan of a big belly, even though people associated having a big stomach with being well-off and living a stable life. In the community where he grew up, people judge one's well-offness via the size and roundness of one's belly. Some people with big stomachs were entrepreneurs, shop owners, and cattle breeders. But he was un-attracted to their lifestyles, and people with big stomachs looked physically unappealing.

They looked too heavy to him, and he always wondered, "How do these people sleep on their stomachs, and how can they breathe normally."

He loved the freedom to roll around on his bed while sleeping, and he could not understand how people with big bellies managed that when they slept and how they enjoyed their bedtime.

"Maybe they only lie down on their back, who knows?" he wondered.

Since he developed the sports virus and started practicing sports activities (jogging, running, stretching, etc.) regularly, he has always done these activities outside of nature. He also works out along the riverbed. The famous Fleuve Djoliba is only one kilometer away from his residence. That allowed him to walk or run up there to stretch, jog, or run. It allowed him to be in touch with nature, breathe fresh air, and enjoy the environment.

The harsh truth one can discover in a sports journey is that you do not like it initially. It is very rare for people to naturally like sport. Our body likes the inactivity and relaxing mode naturally. First, you can do it because you know or heard its benefits. It takes work to take the first step and commit to doing it regularly. That is the main issue. Many say their New Year resolves to start working out, but they cannot keep it going.

One comes to like it by doing it. By forcing yourself to do it, you will get the virus of sport. You will be in love with it by doing it regularly over time. Good wealth comes by drips through patience and hard work, and so does good health via patience and hard work in sports activities and healthy food. To master a skill, one needs to be patient and work hard. It is the same path to being in good shape all around.

The well-balanced, slender man used to hate it with all his might. When he came home from the office, and it was time to work out, he looked at his sportswear in the garage while parking the car. He was frowning and disgusted. He hated looking at the sportswear, but when he put them on and went for sport, he felt lighter, happier, and smiling upon his return. Every time he returns and takes a shower, he feels great.

His mantra is, "Get a little stronger and healthier every single day. Yes, a little stronger and healthier physically, spiritually, mentally, and emotionally."

Working out is part of his everyday life, so he has no health issues. He is literally neither sick nor unwell. He has no difficulty waking up early and generally feels well in his skin. Nothing equals waking up with energy and motivation in the morning. Nothing compares to being comfortable in one's skin and aware of how much one's body can do regularly daily. In addition, being fit and healthy puts life in perspective and improves life in many regards.

When the well-balanced, slender man was asked about his secrets to staying fit and young, he responded, "I manage to exercise discipline in my sports activities." He insisted on the regularity.

"Is it necessary to exercise every single day?" he added.

"Food consumption is regular because we eat every day; sugar and salt consumption is regular; therefore, working out should be regular too," he said.

He insisted, "Make time for sport like you make time for meals, drink, and work."

He said he does everything in his power to maintain good health and do anything he can to adopt a healthy lifestyle. His exercise routine means he avoids a sedentary life. "Physical exercise causes blood flow in the brain, enabling oxygen to access brain cells. Oxygen in the brain cells gives them life," He assured.

He works out double or triple depending on the kind of food he eats and the quantity of sugar or salt he takes in. He believes it is better not to take it in than try hard to get it out through working out. He generally takes half of what he wants to eat because that is what he needs.

He avoids junk food altogether and eats healthy, not necessarily expensive, food. According to him, junk food clogs the arteries and decreases energy, while healthy food gives much energy. He is someone who does not take lightly his sleeping time. He says it is in his habits to go to bed between nine thirty and ten thirty in the evening during the five working days of the week. He feels that not getting enough sleep causes the deterioration of the brain. The length of sleeping time allows the brain to recharge. He also does not smoke, drink beverages, or avoid toxic substances.

The excessive consumption of these substances causes damage to the brain. In addition, he relaxes whenever necessary. He mainly controls his stress level and knows how to deal with pressure. He puts his brain to work. A lot of people practice sports, but they do not know how to exercise their brains. Exercising the brain like the muscle is one of his favorite ways to stay fit and young. Another essential secret of his is to keep loving and spending time with family and friends. Staying in touch with friends and family keeps the brain stimulating, which is paramount. He adventures in the mountains and the parks on every occasion. Adventuring will keep you fresh. And finally, he says, "I am very purposeful; I have a purpose every day and strive to reach it no matter how late and slow."

He insisted that sport and a good diet should go hand in hand. He is not a nutritionist, dietician, or someone who can give you the in and out of food or a particular type of food being good or bad for health. A wise man once used to say, "There are thousands of people who do not do any sport; they have a completely sedentary life; when people have a hold of a little money, they buy a car and drive it all the time. They are not involved in any physical activity. They drive to work, they drive back home, they drive everywhere; once back home from work, they have a sedentary life and only watch TV."

What happens next is that they have consumed all the sugar, salt, oil, calories, etc., that they are supposed to consume in their whole lifetime just in a short period. They become sick and contract various diseases as they age, are less responsive, and are more vulnerable to gems attacks. After visiting the doctor, they return home with a prescription with a long list of medications. The note on the prescription reads this way, "cut out or reduce salt, no more sugar, no more red meat, no more anything with sugar and salt in your food."

The health and fitness you always desire are on the other end of the hard work, self-controlled eating and drinking habits that you despise. So stop hoping for it and start to adopt the health and fitness lifestyles that come with it.

Acknowledgements

I want to thank my father, Elise Kassogue, for being a hard worker, putting the family first in his entire lifetime, and teaching us to be true to ourselves. A big thank-you to my mother, Esther Kassogue, for being the pillar that sustained the family and a caring mother. Stay blessed for giving me a detailed account of the family's history before I came to this world. I am very grateful to my brothers and sisters for showing me their empathy and sympathy while I was growing up and contributing to my upbringing.

I want to give a special thanks to Mr. Gaoussou Mariko for helping me get the prestigious Fulbright Scholarship and for being the first editor of my memoir.

I can never adequately thank my friend Amadomo Kassogue for standing by me during the most trying period of my life.

About The Author

Benjamin Kassogue was born in Danadougourou, in one of the remotest village averaging a 1000 people in Mali. At the age of seven, Benjamin Kassogue went to school in another small village called Pomorododiou, which was close to his birthplace. His dad was transferred there to be the pastor of the local church. He studied so hard and made breakthroughs and went from villages to towns, from towns to cities, from cities to the capital city, Bamako. From Bamako, he traveled to the United States, visited Canada, and followed training in India. He studied English at university and attended the Teachers' Training College in Bamako. In 2015, he obtained the prestigious Fulbright Scholarship to study Curriculum and Instruction at Portland State University, in the USA. As an avid reader, he became inspired by many writers, namely Muhammad Yunus, Jeannette Walls, and Trevor Noah. He started writing in 2019 and *A Pleasant Journey, A Memoir* is his debut book which might be an inspiration to the younger talents growing up in the village with meager resources.

9 7989 89 481217